The Sanctuary and the Final Generation

Dwight Eric Haynes, Ph.D.

LHM, INC.
2603 Artie Street, SW
Suite # 16
Huntsville, AL 35805

10/6/93

ISBN: 0-939298-97-X

Dedicated to
my angel on loan, my wife Eve,
and to our lovely children
Demetra, Samuel, Candace, and David.

TABLE OF CONTENTS

FOREWORD

During my youth M. L. Andreasen was a leading Seventh-day Adventist theologian. He was widely applauded as a perceptive student of the Bible. He was also acknowledged as remarkably competent in the unpublished as well as the published writings of Ellen G. White. His competence in the Ellen White writings was the more remarkable in that her periodical articles had not yet been conveniently republished and, out of deference to living relatives of their original recipients, the Ellen White letters stored in the White Estate archives were still largely off limits to researchers. From his probing investigations in the private collections of elderly brethren Andreasen filled note cards that came to occupy several long file boxes.

As a youth I was aware that Elder Andreasen was an expert in the interpretation of sanctuary symbolism. I was unaware, however, that his presentation of a "final generation" was "Andreasen's view of the final generation" or that it would ever be described as his view. In its essential aspects, what is now sometimes called Andreasen's view of the final generation seemed to me then and seems to me today to be so clearly taught in the Bible and in the Ellen White writings that it should be regarded as the *Biblical* view of the final generation and as the *Seventh-day Adventist* view of it. This evaluation seemed to be shared by my teachers in grade school, academy, college, and Seminary.

Without making any reference to Elder Andreasen, my teachers cited Revelation 12:17, about the "remnant of her seed" who, after the close of the 1260 years, would "keep the commandments of God and have the testimony of Jesus" (defined in Revelation 19:12 as the "spirit of prophecy"). My teachers taught me to memorize Revelation 14:12, about the "saints" who, in response to the judgement-hour proclamation of the three angels' messages, would "keep the commandments of God and have the faith of Jesus." They taught me Revelation 7:1-3, about the special end-time group, the symbolically numbered 144,000, whose characters would be so sealed that they would no longer sin and whom Revelation 14:1-5 described as being "without fault" and as having "no guile in their mouths."

My teachers also used page 69 of *Christ's Object Lessons*, "Christ is waiting with longing desire for the manifestation of Himself in His Church. When the character of Christ shall be perfectly reproduced in His people, then He will come to claim them as His own," and other similar passages.

As for the word "perfect," we found in not so much in Andreasen's writings as in Christ's Sermon on the Mount, "Be ye therefore perfect, even as your Father which is in heaven is perfect." I was never warned that my Saviour's command was a threat to my emotional stability! Instead, I was directed to *Desire of Ages*, page 311, which comments on "Be ye therefore perfect" by saying, "This command is a promise." We did not search Andreasen's books for arguments about perfection for we found the concept, even the word, cropping up again and again as a basic feature of the Ellen G. White writings. Perfection meant Christ-likeness, and Christ-likeness was the most desirable of all goals for anyone who wanted to be a loyal loving Christian.

I have not forgotten the shock I felt in 1962 when a new kind of theologian informed me that "perfection is impossible; everyone knows that." Subsequently I observed that in some quarters quoting *Christ's Object Lessons*, page 69 was proof of heresy! And subsequent to that I heard that any concept of a "final generation" was a denial of the gospel. As if the promise of triumph over selfishness, the promise of maturing into the loving character of Jesus could even remotely be considered a denial of the gospel!

So it was that when Dwight Eric Haynes proposed to

rediscover the beautiful view of a final generation that M. L. Andreasen had once so effectively articulated, I was delighted. Dwight did his work under the guidance--and scrutiny--of a committee of professors at the Seventh-day Adventist Theological Seminary (part of Andrews University in Berrien Springs, Michigan). He developed and defended his thesis very successfully. And in doing his research he had the marvelous benefit of access to Andreasen's impressive collection of note cards that I mentioned a moment ago, a collection now in the hands of Dr. John Baldwin, the chairman of his research committee.

Admittedly, Dwight is not entirely unbiased! Converted to Jesus Christ from a life of rebellion against Him, he gives every indication of loving His Saviour--and of longing to be like Him in every way. I believe that Dwight wants to see Christ's character perfectly reproduced in his own life. He wants to be part of that "final generation."

I trust that Dwight's presentation of the "final generation" in this book will encourage every reader to be part of it.

C. Mervyn Maxwell, Ph.D., Professor Emeritus
Andrews University Theological Seminary
January 1992

PREFACE

Personal Vita

Soon after my family and I joined the Adventist Church in 1983, I formally resigned my Baptist pastorate, eager to study more deeply into the three angels' messages of Revelation 14. Our new-found faith was, and continues to be, a source of great spiritual motivation and insight to me. As a Baptist pastor, I was often frustrated by the disunity within dispensationalism in regard to eschatology. I was a posttribulational premillennialist. After our baptism, two local Adventist elders came to our home weekly for a year and studied with us the "Conflict of the Ages" series in conjunction with the Scriptures. During this period, I noticed a continual reoccurrence of sanctuary language and imagery, with which I was only vaguely familiar.[1]

---

[1]The sanctuary is of little or no importance to a dispensationalist. I was strictly taught the seven dispensational periods of C. I. Scofield, in which the tabernacle is considered as "typical in three ways: (1) of the Church as a habitation of God through the Spirit (v. 8; Eph. 2:19-22); (2) of the believer (2 Cor. 6:16); and (3) as a figure of things in the heavens (Heb. 9:23-24)." See The New Scofield Reference Bible, 1969 ed., Exod 25:9

In my pre-Adventist days, my conservative position as a posttribulational premillennialist[1] precipitated an obligation to address the more relevant issue of the last generation prior to the second coming of Christ. I was often perplexed and frustrated as a consequence of my distorted eschatological perspectives as a dispensationalist.

However, my study of the sanctuary as an Adventist resulted in a broad understanding of the prophecies and the

---

footnote. The sanctuary is not given much attention at all. At best it is an object lesson or illustration with little relevance for us today.

[1]Adherents of the three major millennial views place the great tribulation at different points in time relevant to the millennium: (1) amillennial, which considers the millennium to have no relavence to the tribulation, but considers it to be a purely spiritual reality from the first advent to the second; (2) postmillennial, which views history as moving toward the Christianization of the world by the church. A future millennium closing will constitute the begining of the great tribulation; and (3) premillennial, which sees the great tribulation immediately preceding the millennial period.

Within the premillennial school of thought there looms the vital issue of the rapture. The three major views on the time of the rapturein relationship to the great tribulation are: (1) pretribulational--the rapture is to precede the great tribulation; (2) midtribulational--the rapture is to take place in the middle of the great tribulation; and (3) posttribulational--the rapture is to follow the great tribulation.

doctrines of the Seventh-day Adventist Church. Prior to my baptism into the Seventh-day Adventist Church, I understood several varied portions of prophecy and doctrine, but I was not able to tie them all together. My study of the sanctuary doctrine consolidated the fragmented pieces of prophecy and doctrine into a single panorama of spiritual beauty. In my further study of the sanctuary as an Adventist, I found myself face to face with the issue of the final generation once more. I sensed again feelings of perplexity and frustration; yet I felt confident that, through the aid of the Holy Spirit in my growing insight into the sanctuary and through the study of the Scriptures and the writings of E. G. White, answers were attainable to my old questions. [1]

---

[1]For nine months, while attending Oakwood College, I had the privilege to conduct a thirty-minute television series on the sanctuary on CATV-9 in Huntsville, Alabama. I have been invited to campmeetings, federations, societies, schools, and countless numbers of churches to conduct seminars on the sanctuary. These presentations have been invaluable to me, resulting in many years of study, an eight-tape (two hours each) video series, a ten-tape (ninety minutes each) cassette series, a five-foot long and three-foot wide replica of the sanctuary, a one hundred and three page syllabus, over a hundred overhead transparencies, and a collection of over two hundred books on the sanctuary.

Specific Reason for Writing This M.A. Thesis

While reading M. L. Andreasen's book on the sanctuary, I discovered chapter 21, "The Last Generation." I could not believe my eyes. I felt as if Andreasen had plagiarized my thoughts and the tentative conclusions resulting from prayerful study of the sanctuary as an Adventist.[1] This discovery has prompted my decision to study more deeply into Andreasen's theology of the final

---

[1]Through much prayer and study on the topic of the sanctuary, I was able to draw some tentative conclusions in reference to the issue of the final generation. My findings were based upon bits of information from varied sources and authors. No one book or author seemed to communicate my findings completely. I documented and presented my findings on the final generation to the board of trustees of Oakwood College, the faculty, staff, students, and church members on Wednesday night, February 4, 1987. Elder Woodfork, of the General Conference, Elder Bradford, North American Division President, Southern Union representatives, and all regional conference presidents were in attendance. As the 1986-87 Warren Mosley, homiletic-award winner, I spoke to this board of trustees. God blessed. The findings appeared to be widely accepted and appreciated. I distributed approximately 600 handouts of my presentation entitled "Without Us." The presentation and the remarks of Elder Bradford and others are recorded on cassette tape.

generation, through the lens of the sanctuary.[1]

My current perception of the final generation is consistent with my past impression as a Baptist. I still believe that a person's theology of the final generation inevitably affects how he relates, for example, to temptation, and how one understands the issue of sin. Is it possible to overcome sin in this life? On the other hand, what difference does this question make? Ultimately, a person's relationship with God is affected by how that individual chooses to answers these two very important questions.

Acknowledgments

I wish to make a few brief acknowledgments and to

---

[1]M. L. Andreasen, The Sanctuary Service (Washington, DC: Review and Herald Publishing Association, reprint 1947). Chapter 21 (pages 299-321) is a compendium of M. L. Andreasen's final-generation theology. This is the central place in all of Andreasen's writings where he addresses the issue of the final generation. It should be noticed that it is done only after he has completed his exposition of the sanctuary and its services. Thus, I believe that the sanctuary doctrine is an integral part of his final-generation theology and its development.

thank everyone who may in some large or small way have been of assistance to me.

I especially wish to thank Dr. John T. Baldwin, the chair of the thesis committee, for accepting the topic and the task of guiding this entire project as a scholar and as a personal friend. Similarly, I would like to thank Dr. C. Mervyn Maxwell, Dr. Jon Paulien , and Dr. Daniel A. Augsburger for their dedicated assistance and the time that each of them devoted to the evaluation of the text. I thank, too, Mrs. Joyce Jones for her encouragement and editorial expertise. Furthermore I would like to express my gratitude to the staff of the Andrews University Ellen G. White Research Center, Elder William Fagel, Mrs. Pauline Maxwell, and Mrs. Lucile Haagenrud, where I spent many weeks compiling material for this study.

I am also very thankful for my mother, Eldorado J. Haynes, my sisters, Donna, Kim, and Robin, my mother-in-law, Earlean E. White, and my father-in-law, Pastor J. C. White, who proved to be a tremendous blessing and have greatly supported me in prayer and in other tangible ways.

And finally, I thank my wife, Eve, for her attitude of endless sacrifice, and for her excellence as my personal, private, and pulchritudinous secretary. Also, many thanks to my daughter Demetra for sacrificing her time to baby-sit Samuel, Candace, and David.

Above all I give honor, praise, and glory to God the Father, Christ Jesus the Son, and the Holy Spirit.

CHAPTER I

THE SANCTUARY AND THE FINAL GENERATION: AN OVERVIEW OF THE PROBLEM AND METHOD

> To make it evident that His people are serving Him from motives of loyalty and right without reference to reward; to clear His own name and character of the charges of injustice and arbitrariness . . . God permits Satan in the last generation to try His people to the utmost. They will be threatened, tortured, and persecuted. . . . They are willing to die rather than to sin.
>
> M. L. Andreasen[1]

Statement of the Problem

It is the purpose of this study to investigate descriptively (1) the development of the theology of M. L. Andreasen relevant to his theory of the final generation, and (2) the connection which this theology has with his doctrine of the

---

[1]M. L. Andreasen, The Sanctuary Service (Washington, DC: Review and Herald Publishing Association, 1947), 317.

sanctuary. The following questions illustrate the fundamental concerns of this study, although all the questioning cannot be addressed in the brief compass of this project: How does Andreasen use the sanctuary to lay the foundation for his theology of the final generation? According to Andreasen, why will the last generation be subjected to a time of trouble? Is the time of trouble a form of punishment, or is it a testing period? What is its place in God's salvific plan? Does the Christian church have a distinctive task concurrent with the time of trouble? What is the proper definition of character perfection? Is character perfection set forth as the goal to be reached by all Christians or by a select group? In Andreasen's theology, is the second advent of Christ contingent upon the character perfection of individuals who comprise the final generation? Is character perfection a prerequisite for salvation, and if so, does character perfection become a means of salvation? By what standard and method is character evaluated? Does the final generation constitute the 144,000? What is the significance of the sealing and the post-probationary time of trouble in Andreasen's overall scheme?

All of these questions bear upon another set of questions

of even greater importance and deeper significance: In Andreasen's theology, is the final generation expected to precipitate the ultimate vindication of God by means of character perfection? Was the atonement of Christ complete at the cross, or are there subsequent phases? Why is the vindication of God necessary? Is the vindication of God in some sense paramount to the salvation of the human race? According to Andreasen, why can the vindication of God be accomplished only by the final generation? Does Andreasen, therefore, suggest that there is a possibility that Satan can cause the final generation to fail in its mission of vindication? If so, would this failure of the final generation bring victory to Satan and the loss of all mankind from the beginning of time?

Importance of the Study

Interestingly, the author of Andreasen's biography indicates the importance of the topic of this study as follows:

> Were we asked what we consider M. L. Andreasen's greatest contribution, we would answer, The challenge of the last generation, first presented in *The Sanctuary Service*. May this life story inspire each reader to become part of the

final demonstration to the world of what the gospel can do in and for humanity.[1]

It is interesting to note that the author says Andreasen's greatest contribution is his concept of the final generation which was *first presented*[2] in his book The Sanctuary Service (emphasis supplied). Does Virginia Steinweg mean that this is the first time Andreasen ever presented the challenge of the last generation or that it is the first time this concept was introduced to Adventism?

M. L. Andreasen's theology of the final generation is theologically germane to the essence of what Seventh-day Adventists believe, and it has had numerous ramifications in

---

[1]Virginia Steinweg, Without Fear or Favor (Washington, DC: Review and Herald Publishing Association, 1979), 10. Virginia Steinweg spent many years in researching and writing this book.

[2]To my knowledge, subsequent to my research, M. L. Andreasen was the very first Seventh-day Adventist to put in writing a compendium on the subject of the final generation. Thus, this seems to be the most appropriate place to began an indepth study of this matter of the final generation.

the experience of the Seventh-day Adventist Church.[1]

---

[1]From the 1840s to the present time, the doctrine of the sanctuary, as well as the phenomenological system of the sanctuary, has been of utmost importance to the Adventist Church. The sanctuary doctrine renders the Seventh-day Adventist Church distinct in the Protestant world of theology. As Ellen G. White has observed, "The correct understanding of the ministration in the heavenly sanctuary is the foundation of our faith. The subject of the sanctuary and the investigative judgment should be clearly understood by the people of God. All need a knowledge for themselves of the position and work of their great High Priest. Otherwise, it will be impossible for them to exercise the faith which is essential at this time, or to occupy the position which God designs them to fill. . . .

"All who have received the light upon these subjects are to bear testimony of the great truths which God has committed to them. The sanctuary in heaven is the very center of Christ's work in behalf of men. It concerns every soul living upon the earth. It opens to view the plan of redemption, bringing us down to the very close of time, and revealing the triumphant issue of the contest between righteousness and sin. It is of the utmost importance that all should thoroughly investigate these subjects, and be able to give an answer to every one that asketh them a reason of the hope that is in them" (Ellen G. White, Evangelism as Set Forth in the Writings of Ellen G. White (Washington, DC: Review and Herald Publishing Association, 1970), 221-222). However, concerning this foundational truth, there seems to be a certain inexplicable ambiguity in the thinking of some laity and some leaders in the Adventist Church.

Several Adventists have taken up the task of expounding the subject of character. The following important sources offer varied perspectives: Herbert E. Douglass, Edward Heppenstall, Hans K. LaRondelle, C. Mervyn Maxwell, Perfection: The Impossible Possibility (Nashville: Southern Publishing Association, 1975); Herbert E. Douglass, The End: Unique Voice of Adventist about the Return of Jesus (Mountain View, CA: Pacific Press Publishing Association, 1979); H. K. LaRondelle, Perfection and Perfectionism: A

Perhaps nescience is the root of the problem. At every seminar that I have conducted on the Sanctuary, there have inevitably been several long-time Seventh-day Adventist Church members who have approached me and explained their desire to know how the sanctuary is the 'foundation of our faith' and how the end-time prophecies, the plan of salvation and redemption, the Sabbath, etc., can be seen in the sanctuary and its services. For a detailed account of the development of the sanctuary doctrine in the Seventh-day Adventist Church, read P. Gerard Damsteegt, Foundations of the Seventh-day Adventist Message and Mission (Berrien Springs, MI: Andrews University Press, 1977), 103-177; R. W. Schwarz, Light Bearers to the Remnant (Mountain View, CA: Pacific Press Publishing Association, 1979), 37-63; Arnold V. Wallenkampf, ed., The Sanctuary and the Atonement: Biblical, Historical, and Theological Studies, 3 vols. (Washington, DC: Review and Herald Publishing Association, 1981), 1:516-544.

Dogmatic-Ethical Study of Biblical Perfection and Phenomenal Perfectionism (Berrien Springs, MI: Andrews University Press, 1984), 199-245; Beatrice S. Neall, The Concept of Character in the Apocalypse with Implications for Character Education (Washington, DC: University Press of America, 1983), 145-183; Morris Venden, From Exodus to Advent (Washington, DC: Review and Herald Publishing Association, 1980), 133-190; Colin D. Standish and Russell R. Standish, Adventism Unveiled (Rapidan, VA: Historic Truth Publications, 1983, 1984), 177-229.[1]

---

[1]The subject of consummated eschatology has received differing interpretations within the Seventh-day Adventist Church. One major non-traditional interpretation is presented in the work of Desmond Ford Daniel 8:14: The Day of Atonement and the Investigative Judgment (Casselberry, FL: Euangelion Press, 1980). The author writes: "To even infer that Christ's atoning work at Calvary was not complete but required another phase; to suggest that the merits of the blood of the Savior did not reach the Most Holy Place until 1844; to intimate that our Lord for over eighteen centuries was engaged in a ministry which represented the limited privileges of the Jewish precross era . . . is to imperil the blessed gospel" (p. i).

The following year, 1981, the Biblical Research Committee of the General Conference of Seventh-day Adventists published The Sanctuary and the Atonement;

Biblical, Historical, and Theological Studies (Washington, DC: Review and Herald Publishing Association, 1981), which deals with the sanctuary and the atonement in the Old Testament, Christ's atonement for sin, and His intercession for man in the heavenly sanctuary. Although this book may seem to have been a response to Desmond Ford, many of the articles compiled by Arnold V. Wallenkampf and W. Richard Lesher, the editors, had been written up to three years prior to the publishing of Desmond Ford's book, Daniel 8:14: The Day of Atonement and the Investigative Judgment. Subsequently, the General Conference of Seventh-day Adventists formed a Daniel and Revelation Committee which, the following year, published vol. 1, edited by William Shea of the Daniel and Revelation Committee Series, Selected Studies on Prophetic Interpretation (Lincoln, NE: College View Printers, 1982). Vols. 2 and 3 of this series were published in 1986 (Symposium on Daniel and 70 Weeks, Leviticus, Nature of Prophecy).

Three years after Glacier View, in 1983, another (in addition to Ford's) non-standard interpretation of the doctrine of the sanctuary appeared. In Give Glory to Him: The Sanctuary in the Book of Revelation (Angwin, CA: Robert W. Hauser, M.D., 1983), Robert Hauser states: "The historical approach has served us well in the past, but, like the horse and buggy, no longer fits our needs. This is not to discard the historical approach as untrue. It is, like the horse and buggy, no longer as relevant! . . . The introduction vision in Daniel eight that was sealed had to do with the sanctuary. Also sealed was what would befall the people of God 'in the latter days' . . . . the sanctuary is the key to understanding the book of Revelation! If history tells

Because the issue of the final generation--which we have just entered--in Andreasen's theology is so important, it demands a critical evaluation. Such a study is an appropriate topic for a dissertation on the Ph.D. level. However, preparatory to that task, a precise descriptive study of the development of Andreasen's theology of the final generation is needed, which substantiates the necessity of this M. A. thesis.

Perhaps no Seventh-day Adventist scholar would deny that humanity is definitely living in the final days. In the light of this thought, the discussion of the nature of the last generation, in terms of the feasibility, the probability, and/or the necessity of pre-advent character perfection is one of the major issues confronting Adventists today.

---

us anything it tells us that the scholars of Jesus' day had badly misinterpreted Scripture. I am not decrying scholarship. I would only appeal for a fresh approach to the problem" (Give Glory to Him, introduction). Hauser explains his new approach as "a variant of a subdivision Strand refers to as straight-line, as opposed to recapitulationist. However, in significant ways it differs from the straight-line approach by identifying two areas with dual historical and future applications within the main outline. Therefore, the approach used herein does not fit any of the previous models but is a combination" (introduction).

In Andreasen's studies concerning the doctrine of the sanctuary, he provides us with a clear picture of what he considers to be the victory of the saints and the ultimate triumph of God's purpose. This picture provides new perspective for the motifs, typology, and the free will of humanity, which raises profound questions, as seen in chapter 1, germane to the need of and the very essence of the final generation in Andreasenian theology.

Method of Research

In order to accomplish the task mentioned above, I adopted the following plan of research. I read the following works by Andreasen: The Sanctuary Service and relevant portions of Isaiah the Gospel Prophet: A Preacher of Righteousness, The Book of Hebrews, The Faith of Jesus and the Commandments of God, A Faith to Live By,[1]

---

[1](Washington, DC: Review and Herald Publishing Association, 1928, reprinted Payson, AZ: Leaves of Autumn Books, 1981, 1985, 1986); (Washington, DC: Review and Herald Publishing Association, 1948); (Washington, DC: Review and Herald Publishing Association, 1939); (Washington, DC: Review and Herald Publishing Association, 1948).

Following the Master, Prayer, The Sabbath: Which Day and Why? and Letters to the Churches.[1] Second, I also read in chronological order, beginning with Andreasen's first published article, appropriate portions of articles, correspondence, and relevant quotations in Andreasen's personal Spirit of Prophecy card file. Dr. J. T. Baldwin, my thesis chair, graciously lent me four file draws of M. L. Andreasen's personal card file which contain categorized quotes of E. G. White on 4 x 6 cards written by M. L. Andreasen. General Conference Archives Director, Bert Haloviack, searched the archives for a syllabus of M. L. Andreasen that was used during his teaching career. Haloviack was unable to locate any syllabi, but found trunks marked "M. L. Andreasen's teaching materials." To his amazement, the trunks were filled with Andreasen's personal research material, all very meticulously categorized. Approximately 95 percent of this material consisted of Ellen

[1](Nashville: Southern Publishing Association, 1947); (Mountain View, CA: Pacific Press Publishing Association, 1957); (Washington, DC: Review and Herald Publishing Association, 1942); (Payson, AZ: Leaves of Autumn Books, 1980, 1982, 1983, 1984, 1985, 1986).

G. White quotes typed on 4 x 6 cards plus a few quotes of other Adventist authors. Personally I spent many hours searching for syllabi written by M. L. Andreasen. Flo Cloutze, Librarian of Union College, where M. L. Andreasen was a professor and the president of the college 1934-1938 (Steingweg, Without Fear or Favor, 126-134), searched Union College archives for material, but to no avail. James Nix searched the archives of Loma Linda University Library and was unable to locate any pertinent information. Interviews with Daniel Augsburger, professor of Church History at Andrews University Theological Seminary, and Virgina and Bruno Steinweg, authors of the biography of M. L. Andreasen Without Fear or Favor and former students of M. L. Andreasen, reveal that they do not recall Andreasen ever issuing a syllabus in his classes; they remember him using 4 x 6 cards in the classroom with quotes written or typed upon them. The vast majority of those quotes were from the writings of Ellen G. White. Finally, I consulted what others have written about Andreasen which may be germane to his concept of the final generation.

Structural Composition of the Thesis

Structurally, this thesis is comprised of three chapters. Chapter 1 provides an introduction and a brief, but focused, historical survey of issues relating to the nature of the problem. Chapter 2 constitutes the body of the thesis which (1) addresses the immediate contextual setting in which Andreasen's theology is presented and (2) describes the development of Andreasen's theology of the final generation. Chapter 3 provides a summary of findings in Andreasen's theology of the final generation, the connection made within his treatment of the doctrine of the sanctuary, and makes suggestions for further research.

Brief Historical Survey of Freewill as Background to Andreasen's Final-Generation Theology

The issues addressed in this section on freewill are intimately tied to Andreasen's development of his theology of the final generation. The issue of obedience in Andreasen's theology is a salient factor in the final generation. But, human obedience cannot be properly addressed without significant discussion concerning one's presupposition of humanity's volitional capacity, the freewill of human beings. Andreasen says that "Christ showed the way. He took a human body, and in that body demonstrated the power of God. Men are to follow the example Jesus Christ, the Son of God, and prove that what God did in Christ, He can likewise do in every human being who submits to Him."[1]

Three philosophical positions describe the volitional capacity of humanity: determinism, indeterminism, and self-determinism. Determinism is the belief that all human actions are the result of antecedent factors or causes. Naturalistic determinists argue that human behavior can be fully explained in terms of natural causes. Theistic determinists trace human actions to God's controlling hand. Opposite to determinism is indeterminism, which sees no causes for human actions, antecedent or otherwise. The final position is self-determinism or free will, the belief that human beings determine their own behavior freely and that no causal antecedents can sufficiently account for their actions. Of these three basic views, theistic determinism and

---

[1] Andreasen, The Sanctuary Service, 299.

self-determinism were discussed especially in the early church (by Pelagius and Augustine) and in the Reformation (by Erasmus and Luther). I also briefly consider the view of E. G. White on free will.

Early Church Period

The fulcrum upon which the controversy with Pelagius turned was the meaning of grace. Pelagius and Augustine were agreed that we are what we are by the grace of God. But Pelagius spoke of "general grace" and Augustine of "special grace." Special grace comes from the sacrifice of Jesus on the Cross,[1] mediated through baptism via sacraments[2]. Even in articulo mortis[3] baptism could

---

[1]Jaoslav Pelikan, The Christian Tradition: A History of the Development of Doctrine (Chicago, IL: The University of Chicago Press, 1971), 1:308-313.

[2]In medival theology this concept is referred to as ex opere operato. Muller defines it as follows: "by the work performed; with reference to the sacraments, the assumption of medieval scholasticism and Roman Catholicism that the correct and churchly performance of the rite conveys grace to

guarantee salvation, and in every case brings about a condition in which good works can be done meritoriously. But for unbaptized individuals living outside of grace, no merit is attached to good works.[1] Pelagius (according to his enemy, Augustine) asserted that the general grace of God in the endowment of human nature enables us to do His will, if only we are willing to do it. It is sometimes said that the theological difference here reflects a psychological difference

---

the recipient, unless the recipient places a spiritual impediment (obex) in the way of grace. Sacraments themselves, therefore, have a virtus operativa, or operative power. This view of sacraments is denied by both Lutherans and Reformed, who maintain that faith must be present in the recipient if the sacraments are to function as means of grace; the mere performance of the rite will not convey grace." Muller, Richard A., Dictionary of Latin and Greek Theological Terms Drawn Principally from Protestant Scholastic Theology (Grand Rapids, MI: Baker Book House, 1985, 1986), 108.

[3]That is even after an individual has expired.

[1]Ibid., 313-314, 317-318.

between the "once-born" and the "twice-born."[1] In any course of action, there are three elements, posse (power), velle (will), and esse (realization). The first comes from God and the second from human beings, the finished work being the product of co-operation between God and humanity. That a human being possesses the possibility of willing and effecting a good work comes from God alone and does not depend on human will or other power. Thus, to speak of the possibility of sinlessness is not to praise humanity, but God, from whom alone this possibility comes.[2]

Pelagianism flows from the central thought of freedom.

---

[1]Sometimes this distinction is used in defence of the position that there are two ways to God, equally valid, and the one we tread is a matter of personal need. Sometimes it implies that the once-born are 'second-class' Christians, who do not know the depths of Christian experience, and who are swollen with a false conceit of their own righteousness, instead of God's manifold and great mercies. But to explain away the Pelagian controversy in these terms is to oversimplify and to ignore psychological realities.

[2]John Calvin, Concerning the Eternal Predestination of God (London: James Clarke and Co., 1961), 62-68; Pelikan, The Christian Tradition, 1:313-31.

It rejects the idea that an individual's will has any intrinsic bias in favor of wrongdoing as a result of the fall. Since Pelagius believed each soul is created immediately by God, it cannot come into the world soiled by Adam's sin transmitted from Adam.[1] Before a person begins exercising his will, there is only in him what God has created. The effect of infant baptism, then, is not eternal life (which man has already) but spiritual illumination, adoption as children of God, guaranteed residence, citizenship in the heavenly Jerusalem not made with hands.[2]

Pelagius considers grace purely as external assistance provided by God. He leaves no room for any special interior action by God on the soul. By 'grace' Pelagius really means free will itself or the revelation of God's law through itself or the revelation of God's law through reason, instructing us in what we should do and offering to us eternal sanctions. Because this revelation has been obscured through evil customs, grace now includes the law of Moses

---

[1]Pelikan, The Christian Tradition, 4:314.

[2]Justo L. González, A History of Christian Thought (New York: Abingdon Press, 1975), 2:206-210.

and the teaching and example of Christ.[1]

This grace is offered equally to everyone by God, who is no respecter of persons. By merit men advance in holiness. God's predestination operates according to the quality of the lives which God foresees men will lead.

Augustine, on the other hand, believed that sin originated with free will. Free will implies the ability to do evil. Evil is a voluntary, noncompulsory, self-determined act. With the fall, humanity lost the ability to do good without God's grace, yet humans retain the freedom to accept God's grace. True freedom, however, is not the ability to sin but the ability to do good, which only the redeemed possess.[2] The source of salvation is God's eternal decree, which is unchangeable. Predestination is in accord with God's foreknowledge of humanity's free choice. According to Augustine, both those who are saved and those who are lost are so predestined, and salvation is wrought only through

---

[1]Ibid., 211-215.

[2]Calvin, Concerning the Eternal Predestination of God, 65-67.

Christ's substitutionary death and is received by faith.[1]

There is a sense in which the divergence between Augustine and Pelagius is due merely to a difference of emphasis. Augustine stresses divine initiative; Pelagius, human response. In any real meeting of God and humanity, there must be both. Augustine won, in part, because the Catholic Church, seeing how God is greater than human beings and the divine initiative greater than the human response, felt that his emphasis was right. But ultimately Augustine left no room for human freedom. Pelagius' emphasis was not objective; it did not arise from any denial of the initiative or power of God. Indeed, Pelagius in some ways made more of the power of God than Augustine, for he saw in Augustine's denial of the possibility of sinlessness a derogation of God's power. Pelagius accepted with Augustine the initiative of God, but he wished also to assert human freedom--which he did by his division of any action into "posse," "velle," and "esse."

---

[1]Ibid., 67-69.

Reformation Period

As Erasmus reconciled faith and works, so he reconciled nature and grace.[1] We are free before grace for we can accept it or reject it, though our virtues are the work of God. Grace is offered to us, and by our free will we receive it. If we practice good works for the glory of God, God will reward us.[2] Those who are the farthest from Pelagius, said Erasmus, attribute the utmost to grace and almost nothing to free will--without, however, suppressing free will altogether. They deny that human beings can will good without a particular grace, that they can take a good work and accomplish it completely without the essential and continual help of God's grace. "Man must co-operate with God. The gift of grace is God's, but man's share is the

[1]E. Gordon Rupp and Philip S. Watson, The Library of Christian Classics: Luther and Erasmus: Free Will and Salvation (Philadelphia, PA: Westminster Press, 1953), 170.

[2]Pelikan, The Christian Tradition, 2:218-220.

reception of it."[1] Erasmus logically asserts a human is not condemned save by his own fault, but the will of a human being remains in the last resort incorporating self with the Divine action: "It is a reality, not a sheer illusion, making for liberty, not for serfdom."[2]

Martin Luther, as is well known, disagreed sharply with Erasmus on the question of free will. Luther did conclude that man has some free will. "Free-will is plainly a divine term," says Luther, "and can be applicable to none but the Divine Majesty."[3] But in reference to humanity, Luther has no intention of denying the situation which is experienced as the psychological freedom of the will, that one can choose between different possibilities of action. Least of all does he intend to deny the moral responsibility of humanity for its action. He conceded without question these obvious manifestations of the freedom of the will, because they fall

---

[1]Rupp and Watson, Luther and Erasmus, 49.

[2]Ibid., 256.

[3]Hugh Thomson Kerr, A Compendium of Luther's Theology (Philadelphia, PA: Westminster Press, 1943), 88.

outside the range of his discussion of free will.[1] Luther's theology does not dispute about nature but about grace, and does not ask how we are constituted on earth, but how we are constituted in heaven before God. For Luther, it is obvious that we know very well that human beings are appointed as lords over what is under them, which they have the right and the free will to use, so that these things are at their disposal and do as they wish and intend. But human beings are asking, according to Luther, whether they have free will towards God, so that He, God, obeys and does what humanity wills, or whether it is not rather God who has free will towards humanity, so that human beings will and do what God wills, and cannot do anything except what God was willed and done.[2]

One must be careful to note that a complete distinction between two separate spheres is not being made here. The picture that is being presented is somewhat as follows: Human beings can exercise their will with regard to things

---

[1]Ibid., 88-91.

[2]Ibid., 35-41.

which are subject to humanity, and this includes, in a limited sense, the realm of morality, which we may describe as the sphere of activity of secular righteousness, where the concern is with works. But as soon as we turn to consider humanity in relation to God, it becomes meaningless to speak of free will. In relation to God it is impossible for humanity to be the subject of action, for here humanity can only be considered as receiving, as being acted upon, as being subject to judgment, and as being accepted or rejected. Humanity in the sight of God is not something extra and additional to the world. Humanity in the sight of God defines the meaning of its being in the world, whether humanity admits this or not. Thus, one may make the distinction that human beings have free will, not with regard to what is over them, but only with regard to what is under them, and this takes the form of the right to use, to do, or to set aside, according to their free choice, what lies within the sphere of their capabilities and possessions.

Early Adventist Period

There are basically two extremes which exist within

Christendom in general as well as within the Seventh-day Adventist Church which Ellen G. White says should be avoided when addressing the issue of free will. Great minds of philosophy and theology have attempted to navigate theologically between the Scylla of works-righteousness and the Charybdis of anti-nomianism. Often in her writings, Ellen G. White clearly warns Christian travelers about the dangers of the two perils and the need to avoid extremes:

> There are two errors against which the children of God--particularly those who have just come to trust in His grace--especially need to guard. The first, already dwelt upon, is that of looking to their own works, trusting to anything they can do, to bring themselves into harmony with God. He who is trying to become holy by his own works in keeping the law, is attempting an impossibility. All that man can do without Christ is polluted with selfishness and sin. It is the grace of Christ alone, through faith that can make us holy.
>
> The opposite and no less dangerous error is, that belief in Christ releases men from keeping the law of God; that since by faith alone we become partakers of the grace of Christ, our works have nothing to do with our redemption.[1]

Ellen G. White has basically described the arguments of

---

[1]Ellen G. White, Steps to Christ (Washington, DC: Review and Herald Publishing Association, 1892), 59-60.

Pelagius and Erasmus, "He who is trying to become holy by his own works," on the one hand, and, on the other, the arguments of Augustine and Luther, "Christ releases men from keeping the law of God;. . . . [and] our works have nothing to do with our redemption." Thus, the following observations by John W. Wood are appropriate:

> [1] Ellen White believes in free will. The very idea of freedom of choice was anathema to most of the classical atonement theoreticians. Their determinism required that they view the atonement solely in terms of forensic (or legal) adjustments in the status of candidates for salvation.
>
> [2] Ellen White's concept of free will means that she views the atonement as more than an 'infusion' of merit into an otherwise non-active human elect or withheld from equally non-active damned.
>
> [3] Ellen White's concept of free will therefore forces her to reject double predestination; hence, the status of the elect and the damned is not determined in a single legal adjustment at the cross.
>
> [4] Ellen White's anthropology rejects the doctrine of original sin. No automatic guilt passes on all men in a single act (of Adam); likewise, the guilt is not rolled off again by a single act (of Christ). It is a fallen nature, with hereditary tendencies to sin, rather than original guilt, that makes a 'sinner.'
>
> [5] Ellen White's rejection of original sin removes the issue of 'merit' to be earned (or not earned!) by 'good works' entirely. Her plethora of comments about works not earning merit are not directed primarily toward or against a

legal or sacramental theory but toward a legalistic attitude.

[6] Ellen White's free will concept and historical narrative of the great controversy makes atonement an ongoing process completed in phases rather than in one historical event, the cross; both the incarnation and the cross are necessary.[1]

Andreasen's views on the issue of free will as related to the final generation are addressed in chapter 2. It seems that he successfully navigated his theology of the final generation between the apparent perils of works-righteousness and antinomianism.

---

[1]Wallenkampf, ed., The Sanctuary and the Atonement, 715-716.

CHAPTER II

THE DEVELOPMENT OF M. L. ANDREASEN'S THEOLOGY OF THE SANCTUARY AND THE FINAL GENERATION

> Wonderful as is the power of God to forgive, and much as I ought to and must rejoice in it, when I begin to trust that power to the exclusion of the higher power, that of abstinence from sin, or being kept from sin, I am going in the wrong direction.
>
> M. L. Andreasen[1]

The background provided in chapter 1 regarding the import and the effect of the basic issues inherent in the theology of the final generation makes it possible for this investigation to enter its second phase, namely, a chronological evaluation of Andreasen's written works. The

---

[1]Andreasen, "The Keeping Power of God," Review and Herald, June 18, 1936.

primary purpose of this chapter is to articulate a descriptive account of Andreasen's theology of the final generation and its connection in his treament of the doctrine of the sanctuary as it appears chronologically in Seventh-day Adventist magazine articles,[1] books,[2] personal letter correspondence,

---

[1]M. L. Andreasen wrote literally hundreds of articles. These articles were written for Adventist periodicals such as: Review and Herald, Signs of The Time, These Times, The Youth Instructor, and The Canadian Watchman. I have compiled an index of every article Andreasen has ever written and collected and chronologically organized each one. Chronologically, these range from his first article, "Morning Devotional Study: Patience of the Saints; Commandments of God; The Faith of Jesus," Review and Herald, June 9, 1926, to "What Is Man?," These Times, April 28, 1958.

[2]Seven books were written by M. L. Andreasen. Chronologically they are: (1) Isaiah the Gospel Prophet: A Preacher of Righteousness, 3 vols. (Washington, DC: Review and Herald Publishing Association, 1928), reprinted (Payson, AZ: Leaves of Autumn Books, 1981, 1985, 1986); (2) The Sanctuary Service (Washington, DC: Review and Herald Publishing Association, 1937); (3) The Faith of Jesus and the Commandments of God (Washington, DC: Review and Herald Publishing Association, 1939)--this book was also published in a revised edition in 1949 with a shorter title (The Faith of Jesus); (4) The Sabbath: Which Day and Why? (Washington, DC: Review and Herald

and significant portions of his personal research card catalog files of Ellen G. White quotes.[1]

The following questions are addressed in this chapter: When does Andreasen seem to first advocate concepts of

---

Publishing Association, 1942); (5) A Faith to Live By (Washington, DC: Review and Herald Publishing Association, 1943); (6) Following the Master (Nashville: TN: Southern Publishing Association, 1947); and (7) The Book of Hebrews (Washington, DC: Review and Herald Publishing Association, 1948)--written as a supplement to the Sabbath School Lesson Quarterly for the last three quarters of 1948. See Sabbath School Lesson Quarterly, no. 212, Second Quarter, 1948.

[1]Andreasen was a personal friend of the Baldwin family. "To each one who has so willingly contributed to this book goes our profound gratitude. Included are quotations or information obtained from a personal interview with Gladys Andreasen (M. L.'s second wife), Ida Axelson, Ruth Baldwin. . . ," Steinweg, Without Fear of Favor, 10. Ruth Baldwin is the mother of Dr. John T. Baldwin, chair of my thesis committee. He inherited several of Andreasen's personal books and card files and made them available to me for research purposes. They have proved to be an invaluable resource.

final-generation theology?[1] Is any major or critical theological metamorphosis evident or does Andreasen's position about the final generation, once detected,[2] remain constant? What particular methodological principles did he employ, if any, as substantiation for his theology of the final generation? These questions lead to and provide specific direction for this study of the final generation.

---

[1]Whether or not M. L. Andreasen in his written works, more so in his earlier writings, had consciously formulated his unique theology of the final generation as presented in his book, The Sanctuary Service (chapter 21, "The Last Generation"), cannot be proven beyond doubt, but as seen in this study, there is more than sufficient evidence to substantiate the foundational connections with his matured theological views of the final generation in the earliest of writings.

[2]Andreasen appears to have had a hidden agenda with the intention to bolster yet a more fundamental theological concern. Andreasen's underlying theological concern was the cosmic vindication of God through the relative perfection of a sealed eschatological Remnant, a condition upon which the eventuation of the parousia depends. He may have been influenced by Ballenger and/or other turn-of-the century Adventists who tended to place considerable emphasis upon sinless perfection, a personal cleansing from sin. See, M. L. Andreasen, A Faith to Live By, 48-50; The Sanctuary Service, 14-16.

A Chronological Development of Andreasen's Final-Generation Theology

Defining Andreasen's Final-Generation Theology

For the benefit of the reader, a brief definition of Andreasen's final-generation theology is provided, whereby the following sections of this chapter focusing upon the development of Andreasen's final-generation theology are seen and perceived as a unified expression of that theology.

Andreasen himself offers the best capsulated definition or overview of his final-generation theology:

> At the end of the twenty-three hundred days [1844] a people shall arise who will have light on the sanctuary question, who follow Christ by faith into the most holy, who have the solution to break the power of the mystery of iniquity, and who go forth to battle for God's truth. Such a people is invincible. It [*sic*] will proclaim the truth fearlessly. It will make the supreme contribution to religion in its advocacy of the sanctuary truth. . . . The final demonstration of what the gospel can do in and for humanity is still in the future. Christ showed the way. He took a human body, and in that body demonstrated the power of God. Men are to follow His example and prove that what God did in Christ, He can do in every human being who submits to Him. The world is waiting for this demonstration (Rom. 8:19). When this has been accomplished, the end will come. God will have fulfilled His plan. He will have

shown Himself true and Satan a liar. His government will stand vindecated.[1]

The following three basic sources, written by Andreasen, supply a wealth of information in tracing the development of Andreasen's final-generation theology: "The Christian Life," Sabbath School Lesson Quarterly, 1924, consisting of thirteen individual lessons; Isaiah, the Gospel Prophet, 1928 his commentary on the book of Isaiah; and Review and Herald written in the years of 1926, 1936, and 1937. Six major axioms constitute the developed framework of Andreasenian Theology: (1) the motif of human ability to overcome sin; (2) the motif of hatred for sin; (3) the motif of eschatological patience; (4) the motif of challenge: (5) the motif of dependence; (6) the motif of vindication.

Andreasen's Final-Generation Theology in the 20's

M.L. Andreasen taught theology at Union College, Nebraska, during the years of 1918-1922; he also taught at Washington Missionary College, in Washington, D. C.,

[1] Andreasen, The Sanctuary Service, 297-298, 299.

between 1922-1924.[1] In 1924, while head of the theology department at Washington Missionary College, he was asked by the General Conference of the Seventh-day Adventists to prepare a series of lessons for the Sabbath School Quarterly.[2] The titile of these Sabbath School lessons became "The Christian Life."[3] I claim that this Sabbath School series of thirteen lessons, on Christian growth, Andreasen presents foundational statements relevant to his

---

[1]Steinweg, Without Fear or Favor, 92-98.

[2]The Sabbath School lessons, "The Christian Life," were used during the fourth quarter of 1924. By this time M. L. Andreasen had begun to work as president of the Minnesota Conference (Steinweg, Without Fear of Favor, 98).

[3]To my knowledge, this series of Sabbath school lessons constitutes the very first published works of M. L. Andreasen. These Sabbath School lessons are neither indexed by author, nor do they bear the author's name anywhere in the entire series for the quarter. Virginia Steinweg says Andreasen wrote them and makes the following remarks: "To be sure he [M. L. Anresasen]would not be able to see his students, and they would not even know his name, but he could help each of them to think things through as all around the world they studied "The Christian Life." Internal evidence seems to support Steinweg.

theology of the final generation. While approximately 95 percent of the comments in these Sabbath School lessons are quoted from the writings of Ellen G. White,[1] they constitute his first published words and are helpful in tracing the development of his final generation theology. The use of several quotes in this series depicts Andreasen's perspective on certian issues. They are quotes that he utilizes and expounds in later articles.

1924 Fouth Quarter Sabbath School Lessons

The motif of human ability to overcome sin

In Lesson 2, October 11, 1924, "Righteousness by Faith," in Andreasen's discussion of righteousness by faith, the presentation is dominatedby one particular and very significant principle which later forms a significant aspect of

[1]During these early years in the Adventist Church, the Sabbath School lessons were almost limited to quotes from the writings of E. G. White in conjunction with the Scriptures being studied.

the Andreasenian[1] theology and its connection with the final generation:

> Christ kept the law, and thereby demonstrated that it was possible for man to obey God.[2]

Andreasen's use of this quote points to his belief and support of the idea that human beings can overcome sin in

---

[1]I have coined this term in this thesis and continue to utilize it for the express purpose of identifying that which is essential and indigenous to the final-generation theology of M. L. Andreasen and especially characteristics of his emphasis as distinct from those aspects that were common to Seventh-day Adventists in his day. There are many aspects of Andreasen's final-generation theology that are common in Adventism, particularly as they relate to the doctrine of the sanctuary. His view is also germane to the issue of Christian character perfection. What remains distinct in Andreasen's final-generation theology is the task of this thesis. Andreasenian theology can be marked first of all by its understanding of God's purpose and the magnalia Dei (the mighty acts of God) in the history of mankind all as being relevant to the controversy between God and Satan that originated in heaven.

[2]Andreasen, "Righteousness by Faith," in "The Christian Life," Sabbath School Lesson Quarterly, October 11, 1924, 5.

this life.[1] He further says that "the promise that they 'shall reign in life' does not refer to the future life only. The one who accepts God's righteousness by faith will now have victory over sin and evil, and the future life will be merely a fuller revelation of this."[2] Andreasen's distinct focus upon

---

[1]Within recent years, theological discussion has flourished in the Seventh-day Adventist Church on the subject of perfection. Adventists have been able to approach this subject from an objective perspective, in that perfection addresses the raison d' être, of redemption and reveals to what end God has determined to save sinners. Andreasen's position here is very obvious. Herbert Douglass, Edward Heppenstall, Hans K. LaRondelle, and C. Mervyn Maxwell, four Seventh-day Adventist theologians, have written four representative views of perfection within Adventism that concern this point of Andreasen's and mankind's ability to "overcome sin in this life." See Perfection: The Impossible Possibility (Nashville, TN: Southern Publishing Association, 1975). Many other works by Adventist authors address this issue of perfection as well. To mention a few: Helmut Ott, Perfect in Christ (Washington, DC: Review and Herald Publishing Association, 1987); Carl Coffman, Unto a Perfect Man (Berrien Springs, MI: Andrews University Press, 1969, 1982); LaRondelle, Perfection and Perfectionism.

[2]This is Andreasen's final statement in Lesson 2, [Andreasen], "Righteousness by Faith," in "The Christian Life," Sabbath School Lesson Quarterly, October 11, 1924,

sanctification in his perception of "righteousness by faith" is very clear in that passage. "They *will now* have victory over sin and evil, and the future life will be merely a *fuller* revelation of this" (emphasis supplied). This seems to imply that once an individual accepts God's righteousness by faith, that is, at the point of conversion (the "now"), they will experience some degree of victory over sin in their life. Complete victory --abstinence of sin-- is not realized instantaneously, but as the believer grows and matures in their Christian walk, it-- their acceptance of God's righteousness by faith, justification, and sanctification-- will become more evident.[1] For Andreasen, "more evident" is

---

6, which further articulates his position on man's ability to overcome sin.

[1]For Andreasen, there neither was nor is any excuse for man to sin. "God wanted to teach man from the very beginning that it was not necessary to be overcome by sin. God had provided a way of escape." Andreasen, "Morning Bible Study: The Keeping Power of God," Review and Herald, June 18, 1936. In reference to Gen 4:7, Andreasen states that "Cain need not despair; he need not be overcome. 'Do thou rule over it,' are God's words. This is more than a statement; it is a promise. Man need not be overcome. There is hope and help in God. Sin is not to have dominion over us. We are to rule over it." The Sanctuary Service, 16.

the maturation of the Christian life to the point of overcoming sin in this life.

Why does this matter of humanity's ability to overcome sin in this life appear to be of utmost importance? The apparent rationale of Andreasen's position finds its ground in the following passage:

> The work of Satan as an accuser began in heaven. This has been his work on earth ever since man's fall, and it will be his work in a special sense as we approach nearer to the close of this world's history. As he sees that his time is short, he will work with greater earnestness to deceive and destroy. He is angry when he sees a people on the earth who, even in their weakness and sinfulness, have respect of the law of Jehovah. He is determined that they shall not obey God. He delights in their unworthiness, and has devices prepared for every soul, that all may be ensnared and separated from God. He seeks to accuse and condemn God and all who strive to carry out His purposes in this world in mercy and love, in compassion and forgiveness.[1]

[1]This quote was found in Andreasen's personal card file under the subject of eschatology. White, Christ Object Lessons (Washington, DC: Review and Herald Publishing Association, 1941), 167-168. This single quote, perhaps, best represents the plethora of insight and information available in the writings of E. G. White germane to the basic accusation of Satan that God is an unjust tyrant in imposing upon mankind a supposed perfect law which mankind cannot keep, and then condemns guilty mankind to suffer the punishment of hell. Satan claims to have a better law and

Andreasen, in retrospection, evidently, views the accusations which were made by Satan against God in heaven during the rise of the controversy as being highly significant to his theology of the final generation and its connection to his treatment of the sanctuary doctrine.

The freewill of humanity. Lesson 3, in the same Sabbath School series, is entitled "Obedience." Andreasen quotes Ellen G. White: 'Unless Christ should consent to temptation, He could not be overcome. Not all the power of

---

vows freedom and liberty from God's burdensome yoke to all that will follow him. For further comments by E. G. White, cf. The Story of Redemption (Washington, DC: Review and Herald Publishing Association, 1947), 1-41; The Story of Patriarchs and Prophets as Illustrated in the Lives of Holy Men of Old (Mountain View, CA: Pacific Press Publishing Association, 1958), 1-43; Testimonies for the Church (Mountain View, CA: Pacific Press Publishing Association,1948), 5: 287; Testimonies to Ministers and Gospel Workers (Mountain View, CA: Pacific Press Publishing Association, 1923, 1944, 1962), 466; The Great Controversy Between Christ and Satan During the Christian Dispensation (Washington, DC: Review and Herald Publishing Association, 1950), 395, 618.

earth or hell could force Him in the slightest degree to depart from the will of His Father.'[1] In this powerful quote of Ellen G. White, he rather boldly insists that Jesus Christ possesses a will which personally affords Him the decision, that is to "consent," to willfully yield to Satan's temptation and sin, or to willfully yield to God's law and walk in obedience. In other words, Andreasen believes that when Jesus Christ obeyed, He obeyed because He willed to obey. The will is not solely responsible for the obedience of Jesus. It is the combination of the free will and the sustaining power of the Holy Spirit that results in consistent obedience. Just as Christ was not and could not be forced to yield to the temptations of Satan, likewise human beings, except with consent of their free will, cannot be forced to yield to the temptations of Satan.[2] He has established his belief that it is

[1]White, The Desire of Ages (Mountain View, CA: Pacific Press Publishing Association, 1940), 125.

[2]In this lesson on obedience, Andreasen further substantiates his earlier statement and position on sanctification in the life of the sinner and how, at conversion, the sinner will "experience to some degree victory over sin" (p. 29) as a result of his/her acceptance of Christ Jesus into his/her life and the power imparted

possible for human beings to obey God, overcoming sin in this life. It is evident that the free will supported by the Holy Spirit is extremely important in humanity's victory over sin, in Andreasenian theology.

Obedience out of love. Andreasen was an extremely dedicated student of the writings of E. G. White. In Lesson 3, he addresses the issue of obedience, which is intimately identified as a function of an individual's volitional capacity. Hence, the understanding of the Sitz im leben (the back drop) of the conflict which took place in heaven as described by E. G. White and the basic debate in the historical overview on the free will of humanity provided in chapter 1 is, seemingly, of utmost importance for Andreasen.[1] In the

---

subsequent to conversion. Innate in every conversion experience, Andreasen suggests, is the potential and ability within the volitional capacity of humans to either resist every temptation of Satan, or to fall prey to sin only by consent. Andreasen neglects to address what particular areas of sin he is addressing, i.e., sins of omission, commission, and/or ignorance.

[1]Satan propagates the impossibility of man's obedience despite man's "will" to do good and obey God's law. Satan promulgates God as a notorious tyrant implementing His law which demands death to all who cannot satisfactorily comply

following statement, notice Andreasen's approach to obedience from the aspect of obedience out of fear of God opposed to obedience out of love for God, and his concern with God's character being manifested in contrast to the character of Satan:

> The only obedience worth while is that which comes from the heart. Obedience prompted by fear is slavery. Obedience promoted by love is liberty. 'The exercise of force is contrary to the principles of God's government; He desires only the service of love; and love cannot be commanded; it can not be won by force or authority. Only by love is love awakened. To know God is to love Him; His character must be manifested in contrast to the character of Satan. This work only one Being in all the universe could do. Only He who knew the height and depth of the love of God, could make it known. Upon the world's dark night the Son of Righteousness must rise, 'with healing in His wings.'
>
> All true obedience comes from the heart. It was heartwork with Christ. And if we consent, he will so identify Himself with our thoughts and aim, so blend our hearts and minds into conformity to His will, that when obeying Him we shall be but

---

with sinless perfection. Satan questions the motivation of God's adherents, accusing them of attempting obedience out of fear or for fish and loaves.

carrying out our own impulses.[1]

The heart, mentioned here, is the mind, the seat of the intellect. Christ willed to obey; Andreasen quotes, "It was heartwork with Christ."[2] And if we consent, that is if we so choose, desire, or will out of a spirit of love, then Christ will take control blending our thoughts and our desires with His. The efficacy of His invited participation immerses our will into His fusing our impulses, that when, according to Andreasen's use of Ellen G. White, we act in obedience, we manifest our own will.

The motif of hatred for sin

The free will of humanity is extremely important to Andreasen's theology of the final generation. Likewise, so is obedience a major factor. But, there is yet another aspect which, according to Andreasen, must accompany the free will and obedience:

The will, refined and sanctified, will find its highest delight in doing His service. When we know God as it is

[1][Andreasen], "Obedience," in "The Christian Life," Sabbath School Lesson Quarterly, October 18, 1924, 8.

[2]Ibid.

our privilege to know Him, our life will be a life of continual obedience. Through an appreciation of the character of Christ, through communion with God, sin will become hateful to us.[1]

It is evident that Andreasen believes that humanity can live in "continual obedience" to God out of a heart-felt desire of love for God in this life before the return of Christ. Also, extremely important to Andreasen is the point that sin must "become hateful to us."[2] The relationship between continual obedience and sin becoming hateful to us illuminates God's ability to discern motive. Obedience is external; one's attitude and motive are internal. The scriptures teach that if a man lusts in his heart after a woman, although he does not manifest that lust (external obedience), the fact that he desires (sin is not hateful to him) the woman this internal desire, which only observable by God, constitutes sin (Matt 5:28).

---

[1]Ibid.

[2]The implications of this hatred of sin and the first promise of God (Gen 3:15) are dealt with later in the thesis. Cf. <u>Sanctuary Service</u>, 14-16. Andreasen states rather strongly that "hatred of sin is vital to full salvation. Humanly speaking, no man is safe until he has learned to hate sin as deeply as he formerly loved it."

The unveiling of sin. Andreasen's concerns that sin must become hateful to God's entire creation, and that obedience should not arise out of fear of God but out of love for God, in conjunction with Andreasen's concern for God's character being manifested in contrast to the character of Satan, is clearly seen when one considers the account of the controversy which took place in heaven between God and Satan as delineated in the writings of E. G. White:

> A compassionate Creator, in yearning pity for Lucifer and his followers, was seeking to draw them back from the abyss of ruin into which they were about to plunge. But His mercy was misinterpreted. Lucifer pointed to the long-suffering of God as an evidence of his own superiority, an indication that the King of the universe would yet accede to his terms. If the angels would stand firmly with him, he declared, they could yet gain all that they desired. . . .[1]
>
> Rejecting with disdain the arguments and entreaties of the loyal angels, he [Satan] denounced them[2] as deluded slaves. The preference shown to Christ he declared an act of

[1]A portion of the angelic host deceived by Satan to believe that God's law was unfair and forced upon them, seemingly desired to be free from the burdensome yoke of God's law and desired the supposed freedom offered by Satan. White, Patriarchs and Prophets, 37-40.

[2]Satan denounced the loyal angels who saw no light in Satan's accusation as deluded slaves to the law of God, implying they possessed no freedom.

injustice both to himself and to all the heavenly host,[1] and announced that he would no longer submit to this invasion of his rights and theirs. He would never again acknowledge the supremacy of Christ. He had determined to claim the honor which should have been given him, and take command of all who would enjoy freedom. Great numbers of the angels signified their purpose to accept him as their leader. Flattered by the favor with which his advances were received, he hoped to win all the angels to his side, to become equal with God Himself, and to be obeyed by the entire host of heaven. .[2]

This foolish envy and pride of Satan begins the laying of the basic foundation upon which Satan builds, and the mystery of iniquity is the natural result of his folly. Having been cast to the earth Satan, the father of lies and the accuser of the brothern, successfully recruits Adam and Eve in his war against God's law. Andreasen says, "Adam did not fully comprehend the seriousness of his sin or the result of disobedience."[3] According to the following quote, neither did the angelic host comprehend Satan's work:

---

[1]Satan was the first created and most powerful and honored being of God's creation. He was second only to Christ, the Creator. White, Patriarchs and Prophets, 35.

[2]Ibid., 39-40.

[3]Andreasen, The Sanctuary Service, 9.

God permitted Satan to carry forward his work until the spirit of disaffection ripened into active revolt. It was necessary for his plans to be fully developed, that their true nature and tendency might be seen by all. . . . Until fully developed, it could not be made to appear the evil thing it was; his disaffection would not be seen to be rebellion. Even the loyal angels could not fully discern his character or see to what his work was leading. . . .

He [Satan] had sought to falsify the word of God and had misrepresented His plan of government, claiming that God was not just in imposing laws upon the angels; that in requiring submission and obedience from His creatures, He was seeking merely the exaltation of Himself. It was therefore necessary to demonstrate before the inhabitants of heaven, and of all the worlds, that God's government is just, His law perfect. . . .[1]

As a result of Satan's scheme to undermine and misrepresent God's government, it became necessary for God to demonstrate and manifest "before the inhabitants of heaven, and of all the worlds" that His government and His law are perfect. God must permit sin to run its course for the benefit of all creation, that all might see the sinfulness of sin, which God's creation, at that time, was not mentally or spiritually prepared to deal with.

The inhabitants of heaven and of the worlds, being unprepared to comprehend the nature or consequences of

[1] White, Patriarchs and Prophets, 41-42.

sin, could not then have seen the justice of God in the destruction of Satan. Had he been immediately blotted out of existence, some would have served God from fear rather than from love. The influence of the deceiver would not have been fully destroyed, nor would the spirit of rebellion have been utterly eradicated. For the good of the entire universe through ceaseless ages, he must more fully develop his principle that his charges against the divine government might be seen and their true light by all created beings, and that the justice and mercy of God and the immutability of His law might be forever placed beyond all question.[1]

Hatred of sin is vital. Andreasen's use of this passage contributes to the corroboration of the deduction that his attitude toward obedience and the volitional capacity of humanity was influenced by his acceptance of E. G. White's account of the controversy in heaven. He emphasizes the point that an individual "may resist sin; he may flee from it, but as long as there is a lingering love of sin in the heart, he

---

[1]Ibid., 39-42. Within this quote, note particularly the following implication: "The influence of the deceiver would not have been fully destroyed, nor would the spirit of rebellion have been utterly eradicated for the good of the entire universe through ceaseless ages." The implication here is a specific reference to the first promise of God. According to Andreasen, Gen 3:15, God promised to place hatred for sin in the heart of man, and this "hatred of sin is vital to full salvation." Andreasen, The Sanctuary Service, 15.

is not on safe ground."[1] He goes on to say, "As love of God is vital, so also is hatred of evil. It may be said that our capacity for love of God is measured and balanced by our capacity for hatred of evil."

> Sin is not our friend. We may like sin, but sin has no friendship for us. It will ruin any one who embraces it, and will testify against him. It has no honor, not a single redeeming virtue. Even wicked companions may at times evince some sense of duty and obligation, but sin will strangle its dearest friend and mock its dying victim. It will reduce its most beautiful devotee to a gaunt, disease-wrecked specter, and torture the conscience with remorse greater than a thousand hell fires. It has no pity, no bowels of compassion. The greater one's love for it, the greater the pain and misery it will inflict. 'Ye that love the Lord, hate evil.' Ps. 97:10. That is our only hope.[2]

The ideal of obedience being prompted by the fear of slavery contrary to the idea of obedience as the result of love is obvious. Also, in this same passage, the recurring

---

[1][Andreasen], "Obedience," 8. Cf. Andreasen, The Sanctuary Service, 15, where Andreasen's concept on the hatred of sin is more fully developed. Here it is only introduced.

[2]Andreasen, Isaiah, 308. Cf. Andreasen, The Sanctuary Service, 15, where Andreasen's concept on the hatred of sin is more fully developed.

reference to the need of the manifestation of God's character in contrast to the character of Satan is very clear. The hatred of sin is the adhesive which bonds these two basic characteristics of Andreasenian theology together.

The motif of vindication

Andreasen employs a quote in Lesson 3, "Obedience," which primafacie does not seem to be anything out of the ordinary, yet this quote is intrinsically connected to the ultimate end and the vindication of God in Andreasenian theology:[1]

The foe who in the wilderness had confronted Christ, assailed Him now with fierce and subtle temptations. Had Jesus yielded for a moment, had He changed His course in the least particular to save Himself, Satan's agencies would have triumphed, and the world [the plan of redemption for

[1]It must be pointed out here that this quote can only be clarified later in the thesis as Andreasen's final-generation theology develops further. The concept and the connection utilized by Andreasen in this quote is vital to the motif of vindication in his final-generation theology.

humanity] would have been lost.[1]

The connection that needs to be made in the quote is the association of two things, triumph and loss. Satan's triumph is equated with the loss of salvation for all of humanity. This point on "Satan's triumph" and the loss of salvation for all humanity receives further elaboration as Andreasen's theology develops. There is a connection made by Andreasen on this point of "Satan's triumph" with the following quote: "As Satan influenced Esau to march against Jacob, so he will stir up the wicked to destroy God's people in the time of trouble. And as he accused Jacob, he will urge his accusations against the people of God. He numbers the world as his subjects; but the little company [the final generation] who keep the commandments of God are resisting his supremacy. If he [Satan] could blot them from the earth, his triumph would be complete."[2] The correlation to "Satan's triumpn" is a point of chronology. The

[1]White, Desire of Ages, 486. This quote of E. G. White is extremely important to Andreasen's entire concept of the vindication of God, eschatology, and the significance of the final generation.

[2]White, The Great Controversy, 618.

chronological setting of this scene is the "the time of trouble," which is the title of the chapter from which the quote is taken. In Adventist eschatology, the time of trouble is marked by Dan 12:1, "At that time shall Michael stand up, the great Prince which standeth for the children of thy people: and there shall be a time of trouble, such as never was since there was a nation even to that same time: and at that time thy people shall be delivered, everyone that shall be found written in the book." Therefore, the possibility of victory or triumph for Satan over God in the great controversy is still feasible. This concept is a major factor in Andreasenian theology.

The motif of eschatological patience

Lesson 10 in this same Sabbath School series is entitled "Patience."[1] Andreasen capitalizes on his own concept of patience in the Scriptures. The idea of patience in this lesson seems to be an ordinary application as commonly used. "Patience is a positive virtue, not a vegative one." He, however, has a unique understanding of patience. It means

---

[1][Andreasen], "Patience," in "The Christian Life," Sabbath School Lesson Quarterly, December 6, 1924.

more than simply passive acceptance of a situation devoid of any complaint or resistance. Here is Andreasen's biblical definition of patience: "Its real meaning is to endure, to continue to the end, to keep on. . . It is 'he that endureth to the end' who 'shall be saved.' Matt 10:22." Yet, he does not exclude the other more common uses of the word, for he sayes patience is also "keeping sweet under provocation, of not losing the temper under insult." He mentions many of the Old Testament prophets as being an example of "suffering and patience," such as Moses, Jeremiah, Isaiah, Ezekiel, Hosea, Amos, and several others. "Against great odds and sometimes under fierce persecution, they continued steadfast."[1]

Humanity's mission. Inherent in Andreasen's biblical definition of "patience," he introduces his idea of obligation or concept of task for humanity:

> Those who endure are counter happy. It is not enough to begin--we must also finish. Chirst is not only the author, but also the finisher, of our faith. Heb. 12:2. He is the Omega as well as the Alpha. Rev. 1:8. Christ finished His work, and He wants us to finish ours. John 17:4. Paul had the same wish. Acts 20:24; 2 Cor. 8:6

[1]Ibid.

2 Cor. 8:6 (emphasis supplied).[1]

Notice how Andreasen naturally relates enduring to the end, while he expounds further upon his understanding of patience ("those who endure"). He relates enduring to the end with the thought of finishing. "It is not enough to begin--we must also finish." Clearly recognizing the fact that Christ, while on earth, had a specific mission and responsibility as the Son of God and Savior of the world, Andreasen develops an interesting relationship between patience and the mission of humanity; "Christ finished His work, and He wants us to finish ours." It is imperative to notice the formulation of task for humanity and the fact that He (Christ) wants humanity to finish its work just as He finished His. There does not seem to be any biblically or theologically misleading constructions in his perspective of patience, and at this point, many would surely agree that his perspective of patience is acceptable.[2]

---

[1]Ibid.

[2]The fact that Andreasen's views were published in the Sabbath School Lesson Quarterly, which was then and is currently distributed internationally among Seventh-day Adventists, is a statement of acceptance by the Seventh-day

Andreasen's view of patience is consistent with traditional Adventist teachings. Yet, there is a question that begs to be asked, which, when answered, will provide the sensus plenior of Andreasen's reasoning as it relates to his concept of patience, endurance, and mission of humanity. The question is: In Andreasenian theology, what is the work of humanity and its mission on earth? Andreasen states, "Christ finished His work, and He wants us to finish ours."

The search of the answer to this salient question concerning Andreasen's understanding of what the mission of humanity is begins with his introduction of a fundamental and indispensable concept which is critical and essential to his final-generation theology. In the very next paragraph following his statement, "Christ finished His work, and He wants us to finish ours," he quotes Jas 5:11 as a "good example" of what he considers to be the biblical "meaning of the word 'patience.' " Andreasen, having mentioned several patriarchs, focuses on Job, in particular. He makes the following observations:

Adventist Church. However, this does not mean that the Church understood where Andreasen was headed theologically. What was stated by Andreasen at that time was within generally accepted biblical understanding.

Job was not always sweet. He was sorely tried, and sometimes gave vent to his feeling in rather sharp words. In the narrow meaning of the word [patience], Job may perhaps have failed; but in the larger meaning, that of enduring, of steadfastness, of courage, he was eminently successful. In the darkest hour, he could say, 'I know that my Redeemer liveth.' Job 19:25. And if we continue steadfast, if we endure, if we possess that patience included in the larger meaning of the word, we will be counted happy.

As tribulation works patience, and as the remnant church is noted for its patience, it follows naturally that the remnant church will have special trials and tribulations.[1]

Testing of the saints. In this passage, Andreasen takes another critical step in the development of his final-generation theology. Take note of the transition he makes from the enduring steadfastness of Job to "*if we* continue steadfast, *if we* endure, *if we* possess that patience (emphasis supplied)." Andreasen proceeds from Job to us, and then from us to the remnant church. By the words: "As tribulation works patience, and as the remnant church is noted for its patience, . . ." Andreasen has made a transition from Job, to us, to the remnant church without offering any

[1][Andreasen], "Patience," in "The Christian Life," Sabbath School Lesson Quarterly, December 6, 1924, 24-25.

substantiation to justify his assumed corollary.[1] In addition, he suggests that "it follows naturally that the remnant church will have special trials and tribulations."[2] It becomes clear that Andreasen, when he refers to "special trials and tribulations" of the final generation, relevant to his concept of patience as drawn from Job's experience, is very different

---

[1]The fact that Andreasen was a devout student of the writings of E. G. White explains his assumed application of Job to the remnant church. Although Andreasen lacks appropriate corroboration on this particular point, his conclusions are consistent with traditional Seventh-day Adventist teachings on the remnant church undergoing a time of trouble such as never was upon the earth, when the four winds of Rev 7:1-3 are loosed, the seven last plagues of Rev 16;1 begin to fall, a death decree is issued for violators of the national Sunday Laws, and so on. See Leroy Edwin Froom, The Prophetic Faith of Our Fathers (Washington, DC: Review and Herald Publishing Association, 1954, 1982), 4: 970-971, 1047-1048; F. D. Nichol, ed., "Last Days," Seventh-day Adventist Bible Commentary (Washington, DC: Review and Herald Publishing, 1979), 8: 659; Ellen G. White, Maranatha (Washington DC: Review and Herald, 1976), 265-273; Damsteegt, Foundations, 143-154, 214-219. These references supply what Seventh-day Adventists traditionally teach concerning the final trials of the remnant church in the last days.

[2]Andreasen, "Patience," 24-25.

from the traditional Seventh-day Adventist view.[1] The correlation between the testing of Job and the testing of the final generation is conspicuous in Andreasen's theological concept of the final generation. By virtue of its inherency, the answer to the question of his understanding of what the work and mission of humanity is on earth becomes evident in his concept of the final generation. The concept of humanity's mission and/or purpose on earth by Andreasen in the earliest of his published writings substantiates the development of his theology of the final generation as definitely extant in his very first, known, published works. Although He does not answer this question which strikes at the very foundation of his entire theology of the final generation, in this series of lessons he has, with this issue, laid a complete foundation upon which to build, and he does precisely so in his very next published work. It is important to recognize that Andreasen in his perception of patience and the mission of humanity on earth is, evidently, again referring back to the basic accusation of Satan against God,

---

[1]For further information concerning the traditional Adventist views on the subject of special trials and tribulations, see SDA Encyclopedia, 1975 ed., s. v. "Jacob's Trouble, Time of," and "Time of Trouble."

that God's law is unjust and cannot be kept.

1926 Review and Herald Article "Morning Devotional Study: Patience of the Saints"

In his article, "Morning Devotional Study: Patience of the Saints; Commandments of God; the Faith of Jesus,"[1] written nearly two years after the publishing of the Sabbath School lessons and his very first published journal article, Andreasen quotes the text of Rev 14:12, "Here is the patience of the saints: here are they that keep the commandments of God, and the faith of Jesus." In harmony with the title, he divides the text into three basic sections. The dominant theme and focus of the article is clearly stated by Andreasen--"placing special emphasis on the first section" of the text, "Here is the patience of the saints." In this article, he fully develops his concept of biblical patience, which he mentioned in the Sabbath

[1]Review and Herald, June 9, 1926.

School lesson series in December of 1924.[1]

---

[1]I am further led to believe that perhaps Andreasen had a hidden agenda, because he chose this subject, "The Patience of the Saints," which is extremely critical to his theology of the final generation, above a plethora of issues concerning the deteriorating situation prior and subsequent to the outbreak of World War I in the summer 1914, and the effect it had upon Adventism worldwide. In America, the issue of conscientious objectors and noncombatance was very crucial (Schwarz, Light Bearers, 424-430). "During World War I there was increased suspicion on the part of both the general public and government officials of any publications that might subvert American loyalties and hamper the war effort. To some, Adventist teachings relative to the prophetic picture of the United States in Revelation 13 fell into this category. There were enough complaints about the section in Bible Readings dealing with the United States in prophecy to lead the publishers to revise the section. Since Bible Readings was widely sold by colporteurs, it seemed best to attempt to avoid misunderstanding and trouble" (1919 Bible Conference Transcript, July 17, 1919, E. G. White Estate). The use of the writings of Ellen G. White after her death was a definite concern of the Seventh-day Adventist Church during this time and was one of the central issues of discussion during the 1919 Bible Conference (Molleurus Couperus, "The Bible Conference of 1919: The Use of the Spirit of Prophecy in Our Teaching of Bible and History," Spectrum 10, 1 (1979): 23-57. Cf. Robert W. Olson, "The 1919 Bible Conference and Bible and History Teachers' Council," a paper in the Ellen G. White Research Center, Andrews University, Berrien Springs, MI. Andreasen did not address any of these issues at all in the 1920s; instead,

The motif of eschatological patience

Andreasen begins by deductively suggesting that only after someone has been detained and tried, and amid exacerbation exemplifies a patient spirit, only then would it be appropriate to say, "Here is patience." Therefore, the wording logically indicates that there must have been some type of delay and agitation. His attention is directed to the biblical use of the word "patience," showing that it is not used as one possessing a "quiet spirit," but rather its use is "steadfastness, endurance--patient endurance." Thus, Andreasen offers his own interpretation of the text, Here are they that keep on; here are they that do not give up; here are they that are ready, willing, able by the power of the Holy Spirit to work or to wait, and still keep their faith.

Andreasen, a professor of Biblical exegesis,[1] exhibits a substantial use of scriptural text, yet he leans heavily upon

---

he focused upon what was obviously of greater importance, building upon a well-laid foundation. The theological walls of Andreasenian theology began to rise with his in-depth treatment of "The Patience of the Saints."

[1] See title page of <u>The Sanctuary Service</u> (1937 only).

the writings of Ellen G. White for an understanding of the controversy beyond what is offered in the scriptures, i.e., Isa 14, Ezek 28, and Rev 12. He continues to support his position scripturally with the introduction of a concept, which is critical and essential to his final-generation theology, by quoting Jas 5:7-11, where the quality of patience is spoken of five times by the author with the last reference, the strongest portion of his arguement, to patience being: "Ye have heard of the patience of Job." Speaking of Rev 14:12:

> I take it for granted that patience is spoken of for a reason; that at this time there will be need of patience, and that this Scripture is specially applicable to this people. We must stand before the world as those who endure; who do not give up in the face of trial, or even of suffering. This people will pass through some serious experiences.[1]

Observe the immediate transition from the biblical historical context to "this people, we must stand before the world. . . . This people will pass through some serious experiences." Again he maintains his application of Job's experience to the remnant church. Continuing his discussion on the idea of patience, he directs the readers' attention to

---

[1] Andreasen, "Morning Devotional, 23, 24.

the book of Job where the veritable synergy of his final-generation theology imperceptibly begins to formulate:[1]

> I wish to call your attention to the book of Job. I think there are certain lessons in that book which may be of value to us. I believe the book of Job is written for a specific purpose, as well as other parts of the Bible. . . . The book of Job may have a special lesson and meaning for the last days; . . . essential points in it would be repeated. You remember the happenings in that book. What was it written for? According to the texts in Romans [15:4] and 1 Corinthians [10:11] . . . whatsoever things were written, were written for our learning upon whom the ends of the world have come . . . . it contains principles applicable to this time, happenings selected with a special reference to the experiences God's people [the final generation] are to pass through.[2]

---

[1]As previously suggested, it is difficult to know whether or not Andreasen in his written works, more so in his earlier writings, had consciously formulated and begun to propagate his unique theology of the final generation as presented in his book, The Sanctuary Service (chapter 21 "The Last Generation"), or whether his studies, such as the article being considered, led him to the theology of the final generation, as expressed in The Sanctuary Service; but in any case, Andreasenian theology is definitely present.

[2]Andreasen, "Morning Devotional," 24. From the foundation that Andreasen laid in his very first published works, "Patience," in The Christian Life, 23-25, he clarifies his reference to Job's experience and how he sees it in the

The motif of challenge

Job's experience. Andreasen saw Job's experience as having special relevance for the final generation. Building upon this notion, he cites Job 1:6-12. Satan appears in heaven with the sons of God and God asks him, "Hast thou considered My servant Job, that there is none like him in the earth, a perfect and an upright man, one that feareth God, and escheweth evil?" Satan answers, "Put forth Thine hand now, and touch all that he hath, and he will curse thee to Thy face." Andreasen depicts the challenge Satan has made to God. And God accepts the challenge:[1] "Behold, all that he

---

light of Rom 15:4 and Cor 10:11 as having "special reference to the people of God upon whom the ends of the world have come." Thus, Andreasen believes that the book of Job was written specifically for the edification of the final generation and all that succeed them and that it might be known exactly what God is expecting from the final generation.

[1]This challenge by Satan, which had been accepted by God, and which is further expounded in this chapter, functions as an isolated scenario of the time of trouble. For Seventh-day Adventists, the time of trouble specifically refers to that time in eschatology when Jesus Christ, the High Priest of the Heavenly Sanctuary, shall complete His

hath is in thy power; only upon himself put not forth thine hand. So Satan went forth from the presence of the Lord." Disaster comes.

Satan was beaten.[1] He had charged that Job served God because it was paying him; that God had put a hedge about him; that Satan could not get at him. But Job stood the test.[2]

Though Satan was beaten, he was not discouraged and,

---

mediational work for mankind and the sealing of those elected to endure time such as never has been before upon the earth, when the angels of God will be instructed to release the winds of strife, the seven last plagues will fall, and probation for all mankind will be closed, and Satan will deceive the world. White, Great Controversy, 613-634.

[1]In this challenge between God and Satan, there is no stalemate. One will triumph and one will suffer defeat, and so likewise in the final generation there will be no stalemate. One will triumph and one will suffer defeat.

[2]Andreasen, "Morning Devotional," 24. Having lost all of his children, Job "rent his mantle, and shaved his head, and fell down upon the ground, and worshiped" God (Job 1:20). Job was grieved at the loss, but in spite of the calamity he said, "The Lord gave and hath taken away; blessed be the name of the Lord. In all this Job sinned not, nor charged God foolishly" (Job 1:21-22). Satan had charged and challenged God. In the final generation God will meet the charge and challenge of Satan and, as Job, the final generation will sin not, but bless the name of the Lord.

thus, he returns again. Again God asked Satan if he has noticed his servant Job. Satan answers, "Skin for skin, yea, all that a man hath will a man give for his life. But put forth Thine hand now, and touch his bone and his flesh, and he will curse Thee to Thy face." Again, says Andreasen, God accepts the challenge, "Behold, he is in thy hand, but spare his life" (Job 2:1-6). Notice, the only restriction placed on Satan is that he was not allowed to take the life of Job. Satan physically assaults Job.[1] Again, patience, steadfastness, and the endurance of Job was manifest.

Satan was beaten again. He had tormented Job, causing him intense suffering; but Job had stood the test.[2] God's

[1]This scenirio parrallels that of the final generation in that Satan is given full regin over them when the angels of God loose the winds of strife. Likewise, in this situation Satan will have but one restriction placed on him; he will not be allowed to take their lives.

[2]Job, yet unaware of this vital challenge and why he was experiencing so much intense suffering, said, "Though He slay me, yet will I trust in Him" (Job 13:15). This was the defeating blow to Satan's accusations. Job by the power of his own will obeyed God's law out of his love for God, not out of fear or gain of earthly possessions.

confidence in him was not misplaced. . . .[1] He did not know the challenge that had gone forth. God was depending upon him.[2] Job was perplexed. He could not understand why

---

[1]What Andreasen is saying here is that God had been observing Job's actions, his thoughts, and, more importantly, his motives, as only God can do. As it is seen later in this chapter, Andreasen believes that the observing of Job's life, which is not anything out of the ordinary for God because He sees and knows all, is in harmony with God's invitation to Satan in Job 1:8, "Hast thou considered my servant Job?" It shows God's confidence in Job and permits Satan to have his way with Job, because God is confident that Job will stand the test. It is a foretaste of what and how the last events of earth's history shall take place. It is Andreasen's perspective of the sealing of God's people as "all who have proved themselves loyal to the divine precepts have received 'the seal of the living God.' " White, The Great Controversy, 613. Cf. 605. God, having observed the actions, thoughts, and motives of his people, selects only those that possess an attitude that would rather die than sin. As Job said, "Though He slay me, yet will I trust in Him" (Job 13;15). They will receive God's seal and endure Satan's entire control of the final impenitent after the Holy Spirit has been withdrawn from the earth.

[2]Andreasen says "God was depending upon him [Job]." For Andreasenian theology, this is a very crucial point. Satan accuses God, bringing God's government, His law, His character, and God Himself into question. God invites Satan to try Job. Satan challenges God to remove the hedge from around Job and he will make Job curse Him to His

this thing had come. . . . he did not understand how important it was in God's plan that he should stand the test . . . .[1]

He went through the same experience that I suppose every one has gone through, or will go through, before the end.[2]

Final generation's experience. Recounting the experience of Job, Andreasen makes the transition from Job's experience when Satan was given the permission to try him to the utmost to the experience of "the saints when

---

face. God accepts Satan's challenge and unbeknown to Job, God is depending upon him to wreck Satan's attempt to vitiate God's character. Andreasen later transfers and applies this dependence of God upon Job to the final generation.

[1]It was, according to Andreasen, very important to God that Job stand the test, but with the final generation it will be even more important to God, because Christ will have left his work in the Most Holy Place of the Heavenly Sanctuary (White, The Great Controversy, 614). Although Andreasen does not comment on the consequence involved if Job would have failed the test, and Satan had been victorious in his challenge to God, the issue of consequence should failure accrue in the final generation is paramount in Andreasen's theology of the final generation.

[2]Andreasen, "Morning Devotional," 24.

probation shall cease"[1] and Satan, as he was with Job, will be given the permission to try them, the final generation, to the utmost. The winds of strife will be loosed and the world will experience a time of trouble such as never before in earth's history.

> Now comes the challenge. Satan is given permission to try God's people to the utmost. They will suffer weariness, delay, and hunger. They cry to God day and night. It is the time of Jacob's trouble. . . . The people go through somewhat the same experience that Job went through. His experience is written that we may know that there is something going on in heaven, that there is a challenge, that there is a test, and that God is depending upon us to do right.[2]

As previously mentioned, Andreasen makes this decisive transitional correlation between his stated paragon, Job, and the final generation. In this concept of God's "dependance upon us," the final generation, those that have received "the seal of the living God," God has placed His confidence in

---

[1]The close of probation is marked by the irrevocable decree of Rev 22:11, "He that is unjust, let him be unjust still. . .; and he that is righteous, let him be righteous still. . . . " The saints referred to by Andreasen, therefore, must be the final generation.

[2]Andreasen, "Morning Devotional," 25.

those whom He has observed according to their action, thoughts, and their motives. In this select group, according to Andreasen, God will have witnessed the full manifestation of His very first promise to mankind in Gen 3:15 to place hatred of sin in the heart of man. "Hatred of sin is vital to full salvation,"[1] Andreasen is convinced that "humanly speaking, no man is safe until he has learned to hate sin as deeply as he formerly loved it. . . . This combination of love and hatred must be in every Christian."[2] In Andreasenian theology, the final generation will possess a love for and, equally, a hatred for sin, whereby they would rather die than yield to sin that which caused their beloved creator to vicariously suffer death on the cross of calvary. This issue of God's dependence upon the final generation is addressed later in this chapter as it is developed by Andreasen.

The motif of dependence

Inherent in Andreasen's theology of the final generation are two fundemental ideas: first, the idea of challenge and,

---

[1] Andreasen, Sanctuary Service, 14-15.

[2] Ibid.

second, the idea of dependence. Andreasen expresses the idea of challenge in that God has been accused by Satan and, consequently, God has been challenged by Satan to defend and vindicate His name, character, and law. Andreasenian theology is consistantly retrospective in its assessment of all eschatological events. He sees God meeting this challenge of Satan in "the time of Jacob's trouble," which constitutes the final generation of earth's history:

> The keeping of the commandments presupposes perfection, and that is holiness, that is sanctification. Do they keep the commandments to be saved? No, not at all. They keep them because they love. Love is the mainspring, love is the center of their experience.[1]

He expresses his understanding of what constitutes the meeting of the challenge and the vindication of God primarily as the keeping of the commandments of God in perfect obedience out of love for God by humanity. Notice his emphasis upon "love." "Love is the mainspring," it is not a legalistic observance of the law. Andreasen asks the question, "do they keep the commandments to be saved?" He answers with an emphatic "no, not at all. Love is the center of their experience." He further clarifies his position

[1]Ibid, 26.

on legalism: "Now count up your righteousness. . . . prompt in tithe paying, . . . correct in conduct. . . ." After listing a host of things Andreasen says, "all these are good. . . but are you trusting in these for salvation? Without Christ all these avail nothing."[1] This clearly defines his position on the issue of justification by faith, the imputed merits of Christ Jesus as our means of salvation. Yet, the believer's response is one of obedience out of love for the Savior.[2] This, then, dismisses and falsifies the accusations made by Satan in heaven. Andreasen addresses and initiates the development of the idea of dependence, which he only introduces in this article, in several literary sources to be analyzed in the following section.

---

[1]Andreasen, Isaiah, 341.

[2]Although here Andreasen does not employ the term "imputation" it seems that he is using a forensic and judical connotation of the imputed merits of the death of Christ by God in respect the repentant believer, by grace through faith are we saved not by works of the flesh. Yet, the impartation of the righteousness of Christ, obedience, is, for Andreasen, concomitant in the justified believer. Cf. above 50-53.

1928-1929 Sabbath School Lesson Helps
Isaiah, the Gospel Prophet

The last works of Andreasen's to be considered during the 1920s are the three books he wrote as study helps to the Sabbath School Lessons on the book of Isaiah.[1]

The motif of eschatological patience

The first clues in Andreasen's commentary on Isaiah that reveal the development of his theology of the final generation are in his personal commentary of Isa 11:10, 12: "And in that day there shall be a root of Jesse, which shall stand for an ensign of the people; to it shall the

---

[1]Three volumes were in this interesting series, one for each of the last two quarters of 1928 and the first quarter of 1929, as additional material for the Sabbath School lesson. They have been bound into one single volume with the three quarterlies which they augment and entitled Isaiah, The Gospel Prophet. In this commentary on the book of Isaiah, Andreasen utilizes the following format: (1) Lesson Scripture, where he covers the scriptural context; (2) notes, which are exegetical, focusing upon a particular word or a phrase and expounding etymological and cultural insights; and (3) lessons for the day, where Andreasen employs his theological acumen to share his commentary on Isaiah for Christians of today. As he provides information in this section, his observations and interpretation of the text proves beneficial to the comprehension of Andreasenian theology.

Gentiles seek. . . ." Andreasen states:

> An ensign is a banner. . . . On the banner of the remnant is inscribed: 'Here is the patience of the saints: here are they that keep the commandments of God, and the faith of Jesus.' Rev. 14:12. (See "Testimonies," Vol. VII, p. 150.) Christ is our example. The determination of Antichrist to carry out the rebellion he began in heaven will continue to work in the children of disobedience. Their envy and hatred against those who obey the fourth commandment, will wax more and more bitter. But the people of God are not to hide their banner. They are not to ignore the commandments of God, and, in order to have an easy time, go with the multitude to do evil.- Testimonies, Vol. IX, p. 230. [1]

In this quote Andreasen reemphasizes the importance of his concept of patience[2] and its correlation to the final generation in that the banner carried by the final generation is a testimony of the "patience." Notice that the manifestation of Satan's rebellion on earth, which he began in heaven, is continued on earth "in the children of disobedience." They envy and hate those who "obey." The idea of patience and obedience are synonymous in this context. "The people of God are not to hide their banner, they are not to ignore the

---

[1]Andreasen, Isaiah, the Gospel Prophet, 36.

[2]Andreasen capitalizes on the concept of patience in his article, "Morning Devotion," 23-26.

commandments of God, and, in order to have an easy time, go with the multitude to do evil."[1] Thus, a direct association between his Sabbath School lesson on "Patience"[2] and his article on "The Patience of the Saints"[3] is all paramount in the development of Andreasen's theology of the final generation.

The motif of dependence

Witnesses for God. Andreasen employs, as a general heading for Isa 43, "The Gathering of Israel--Witnesses for God." He says of Isa 43:8-28 that the Prophet Isaiah "brings clearly to view one of his fundamental teachings, namely, that God's people are his witnesses." Andreasen further emphasizes the fact that "the significance of this

---

[1]Andreasen, Isaiah, the Gospel Prophet, 36.

[2][Andreasen], "Patience," in "The Christian Life," 24-25.

[3]Andreasen reemphasizes his concept of patience while continuing to build upon the framework of his final-generation theology. "Morning Devotion," 23-26.

should not escape us."[1] Witnesses, Andreasen explains, presupposes a trial, but who is on trial? Andreasen states, "The question at issue here is: 'Who is the true God?' " According to Andreasen, God is on trial; "The hour of His [God's] judgement is come" (Rev 14:7). God is on trial, He has been accused, and He will gather together Israel from the four corners of the earth as His witnesses.[2] He makes the following remarks concerning the witnesses:

> On the testimony of these witnesses hangs the case. A witness may tell only that which he knows. He may not relate hearsay. He may not preach a sermon. He may strictly adhere to the one thing only: his own experience. If you were put on the witness stand and restricted to these rules, how would you prove God to be the true God?[3]

Upon witnesses the case hangs. Andreasen's concept that the vindication of God depends on the testimony of human witnesses is vital to his mature final-generation theology, as we shall see as we proceed: "On the testimony of these witnesses hangs the case," is unequivocally the last nail in the developmental framework of Andreasen's final-

---

[1] Andreasen, Isaiah The Gospel Prophet, 161.

[2] Ibid., 161-168.

[3] Ibid., 161.

generation theology. The context is the eschaton. God is on trial and the entire case shall be decided upon the testimony of God's witnesses which have been gathered from the four corners of the earth, the final generation.[1] Then Andreasen asks a question, "How would you prove God to be the true God?" He offers no answer other than, "Whatever God sets out to do, that he does. God will finish His work in the earth on time. Rom 9:28. None [this includes Satan and all of his agencies] can hinder Him."[2]

The concept of dependence in Andreasen's theology at this point is in its embryonic stage. Thus far, he has established and documented his stated belief of God's dependence upon Job and, likewise, His dependence upon

---

[1]Basically, the natural end of Andreasen's theological concept of the final generation is evident in this section of his commentary on Isaiah. His ideas of challenge, patience, man's work on earth, and, most importantly, his idea of God's dependence upon the final generation joins together in his conclusion that "upon the testimony of these witnesses [the final generation] hangs the case" of God's final and ultimate vindication.

[2]Ibid., 167. There are several other quotes in Andreasen's commentary on Isaiah relevant to the development of Andreasen's theology of the final generation. See pp. 285-287, 307-317.

the final generation in the conflict between God and Satan. He has not, yet, elaborated upon the issue concerning to what extent God, the Supreme Being, is dependent upon the final generation. Andreasen's synergistic concept of dependence grows and develops to its fruition in the 1930s.[1]

Andreasen's Final-Generation
Theology in the 30s

1936 Review and Herald Article
"The Keeping Power of God"

Most of Andreasen's years in the 1930s, from 1931 to 1938, were spent at Union College as professor and president. The article "The Keeping Power of God" was published in the Review and Herald, June 18, 1936, while Andreasen was president of the College. The basic thrust of this writing is that "it is just as important to learn to hate sin as it is to learn to love righteousness. . . ."[2] He goes on to say that hatred for sin is a "part of the plan of God. . . ." He stresses the point of the hatred of sin

[1] Andreasen, The Sanctuary Service, 299-334.

[2] Andreasen, "Keeping Power of God," 16.

being "fundamental to Christianity."

The motif of hatred for sin

God's first promise. This concept of the hatred of sin is mentioned by Andreasen in his 1924 Sabbath School series where he states that "through an appreciation of the character of Christ, through communion with God, sin will become hateful to us."[1] He does not develop this thought in the Sabbath School series. Nearly twelve years later in his article, "The Keeping of God," he explicates this idea and reveals its affinity to his final-generation theology. The article begins by depicting God, after Adam had sinned and hid himself, walking through the garden in the cool of the day searching for man. In Gen 3:9, "And the Lord called unto Adam, and said unto him, Where art thou?" Andreasen then focuses on Gen 3:15, "I will put enmity between thee and the woman, and between thy seed and her seed." He interprets this text "not merely as a statement but as a promise."[2] He paraphrases the text to say, "I

---

[1][Andreasen], "Obedience," in "The Christian Life," 6-9.

[2]Andreasen, "The Keeping Power of God," 16.

will put hatred into your heart for sin."[1] The fact that he sees this text as a promise is important, because as a promise God then obligates Himself to place the hatred of sin in the hearts of all who desire to follow Him.

Hatred of sin a part of God's plan. Thus, Andreasen, as is seen later, believes that God, having made this promise expects, this hatred of sin from every Christian. That is why he considers the "hatred of sin" as "fundamental to Christianity."[2] Adam had sinned against God, but without doubt did not fully understand what sin meant. God killed animals to clothe Adam and Eve. This obviously was the first time Adam or Eve had ever seen death, "and when he saw the first slain lamb, it must have come to him with fuller significance than in any other way that sin means death."[3]

---

[1]Ibid.

[2]Ibid.

[3]Ibid. After sin marred this fair world, nature everywhere revealed the presence and the character of the evil one. "The atmosphere, once so mild and uniform in temperature, was now subject to marked changes (White, Patriarchs and Prophets, 61). Satan had become the prince of the air (Eph 2:2). When Adam and Eve witnessed signs of death and decay in the drooping flowers and the leaves

The skins of these animals that they saw slain to cover their nakedness were to be not only their garments but "a continual reminder to [them] of [their] sin."[1] God was desirous then and now to inculcate this rudimentary principle and fact that sin, the transgression of God's law, equals death. Therefore, the hatred of sin "I conceive to be a part of the plan of God."[2] He utilizes the statement of Gen 3:15 as a promise, as a harbinger, that suggests naturally of its constitutional position as a part of the plan of God. "It is only when we learn to hate the sin that kills and destroys and pollutes, only then are we on safe ground. This hatred toward sin," Andreasen says, "I consider fundamental to Christianity."[3] There are two basic points in the first few chapters of Genesis, according to Andreasen, that

---

falling from the trees, we are told that they "mourned more deeply than men now mourn over their dead" (White, Patriarchs and Prophets, 62).

[1]Andreasen, "The Keeping Power of God," 16.

[2]Ibid.

[3]Ibid. It becomes very obvious why "hatred of sin" was considered as "fundamental to Christianity" in Andreasen's theology of the final generation.

summarize the entire gospel: (1) That God initiates the search for lost and sinful humanity and (2) that God vividly provides His prize creation with a visible object lesson clearly revealing the essence of sin--death. In conjunction with this revelation, God promises, in Gen 3:15, to place "in the sinner's heart--who desires to turn from sin--hatred of sin."[1]

The motif of human ability to overcome sin

No excuse for sin. God endeavored to inculcate, according to Andreasen, this foundational principle from the very beginning that "it was not necessary to be overcome by sin." He uses as substantiation, "Do thou rule over it."[2]

---

[1]Ibid.

[2]"The Keeping Power of God," 16. Andreasen supplies only the last clause of Gen 4:7, "Do thou rule over it," without any reference as to the verse quoted or the particular translation used. He utilizes this same quote in The Sanctuary Service, 16, and documents his use of Gen 4:7 RSV. This verse presents certain linguistic problems, i.e., "And unto thee shall be his desire, and thou shalt rule over him." The interpretation of the third person personal pronoun "his" has great bearing upon one's perception of

Advancing his position that Adam, nor any human being, had or has any excuse to sin, Andreasen makes the following comments:

> It is the same lesson that God sought to teach Israel later on in the sacrificial system, when the priests stood there day by day, ministering in and with blood. God wanted them to receive through that ministration an abhorrence for sin. By no stretch of the imagination can one ever believe that it is pleasant work to minister with blood, to dip the hand into it, to work with it all the day long. God wanted not only to teach Israel that, under sin, death ensues, but also to teach His ministers, and people, all of them, abhorrence for sin, so that they would go and sin no more.

God's statement. There are three contrasting views of the interpretation of this pronoun among many commentators: "(1) Abel's (LXX. (?), Chrysostom, Ambrose, Grotius, Calvin, Ainsworth, Bush, Speaker's, Bonar, Exell); or (2) sin's (Vulgate (?), Luther, Rosenmüller, Von Bohlen, Kalisch, Keil, Delitzsch, Murphy); or (3) the sin offering's (Faber, Candlish)" ("Genesis," The Pulpit Commentary, ed. H. D. M. Spence and Joseph S. Exell [Grand Rapids, MI: Eerdmans Publishing Company, 1980], 1:79). The first and the third interpretations have been eliminated by empirical observation, exegesis. The difficulty in translating ('ghat-tahth') is very well explained in comments on Gen 4:7. See "Genesis," SDA Bible Commentary, 1:240, which recommends the RSV translation, "you must master it," which is worded slightly different from the RSV translation in use at that time by Andreasen, but both translations carry the same connotation.

> I wish to emphasize that. The sacrificial service, wonderful as it was, was not intended to be permanent. It was a lesson to teach man that sin means death, and to teach him abhorrence for sin-really, in the words of Christ, 'Go, and sin no more.'[1]

A higher power. Following his argument, Andreasen with theological lucidity brings to bear what he considers "the prophetic message all the way through the Old Testament, 'Behold to obey is better than sacrifice.' "[2] Not only does he regard this as the all-encompassing prophetic message of the Old Testament, but Andreasen correspondingly sees this message as the tenor of the New Testament. "To obey is better than sacrifice," according to Andreasen, is elucidated "in the words of Christ addressing the woman caught in adultery, 'Go and sin no more.' "[3] Thus, for Andreasen, this message postulates the main focus of the entire Bible and God's plan of redemption for humanity. He drives the point home with this statement:

> There is no more beautiful doctrine than forgiveness of sins. If I sin, however dark that sin may be, I can be

[1] Andreasen, "The Keeping Power of God," 16.

[2] Ibid.

[3] Ibid.

forgiven. There is cleansing in the blood of the Lamb. If I sin once, twice, seven times, seventy times seven, God will forgive. But the moment I begin to trust to the forgiving power of God apart from that greater power, the keeping power of God, I am on the wrong track. Let me repeat that: Wonderful as is the power of God to forgive, and much as I ought to and must rejoice in it, when I begin to trust that power to the exclusion of the higher power, that of abstinence from sin, or being kept from sin, I am going in the wrong direction.[1]

The first relationship drawn between the final-generation and sanctuary

The functionality of the inner court. The juxtaposition of God's keeping power, the sanctuary, the final generation, and the conclusions that Andreasen draws from the relationship existing among these three entities is Andreasen's closing motif of this article. He has explicated his position on the keeping power of God, i.e., its superiority over God's power to forgive. Recounting the earthly Israelite cultic sacrificial system, Andreasen refers to the first apartment of the Old Testament sanctuary, that is, the Holy Place, citing it as the place where the blood, the medium through which sin was transferred into the

---

[1]Ibid.

sanctuary, was carried by the officiating priest and forgiveness was secured.

On the tenth day of the seventh month, the day of atonement, the ministry of the officiating priest, the high priest, was conducted in the second apartment, the Most Holy Place, where sin was blotted out. Therefore, Andreasen makes the deduction that "the first [apartment] stands for forgiveness, [and] the second [apartment] for blotting out [of sin]."[1] The delineation of Andreasen's idea of God's keeping power is clearly seen in his interpretation that the blotting out of sin includes complete victory over it, according to his compartmental depiction of the forgiveness of sin as indigenous to the Holy Place and the blotting out of sin accomplished in the Most Holy Place of the sanctuary. Having quoted several paragraphs from Early Writings,[2] he makes the following observations:

> This chapter has been much misunderstood and used by our enemies, and I am afraid that because of that we have neglected to read it as we should; but, friends, there are wonderful lessons here. God wants us to pass from the first

---

[1]Ibid.

[2]White, Early Writings, 54-56. The title of this chapter, from which Andreasen is quoting, is "End of 2300 Days."

to the second apartment, the first standing for forgiveness, the second for the blotting out of sins. Wonderful as is the doctrine of forgiveness, there is a still higher power, that of keeping from sinning.[1]

It is highly significant to note the correlativity of the power of God's forgiveness of sin in the Holy Place and God's transcendent power of abstinence from sin in the Most Holy Place. When Andreasen says that "this chapter [End of The 2300 Days] has been much misunderstood" and misapplied, he seems to be referring specifically to one's understanding of the distinct difference of function between the first and the second apartments, as he explained.

In Andreasen's explanation of the end of the 2300-day prophecy and its relationship to those on earth, his interpretation as to the significant difference in functionality between the first and second apartments had been gravely misunderstood, according to Andreasen, by many Seventh-day Adventists at that time.[2] With the idea in mind of God's

---

[1]Andreasen, "The Keeping Power of God," 17.

[2]A host of Adventist authors address the issues of the heavenly sanctuary, the 2300-day prophecy, and Christ as our High Priest. However, the focus these authors appears to be directed toward something other than the

compartmentalized concept of God's power to forgive sin (the Holy Place) and God's transcendent power of abstinence from sin (the Most Holy Place); i. e., Frank B. Holbrook, for example see the following excellent studies, Symposium on Daniel, Daniel and Revelation Committee Series (Washington, D C: Biblical Research Institute, 1986), 2:428-496; William H. Shea, Selected Studies on Prophetic Interpretation, Daniel and Revelation Committee Series (Washington, D C: Biblical Research Institute, 1982), 1:132-137; Edward Heppenstall, Our High Priest (Washington, D C: Review and Herald Publishing Association, 1972), 49-186; C. Mervyn Maxwell, God and His Sanctuary (Mountain View, CA: Pacific Press Publishing Association, 1980), 28-38; C. Mervyn Maxwell, Perfection: The Impossible Possibility, 154-174; F. C. Gilbert, ed., Practical Lessons (Nashville, TN: Southern Publishing Association, 1972), 285-308; Norman R. Gulley, Christ Our Substitute (Washington, D C: Review and Herald Publishing Association, 1982), 112-127; Morris Venden, From Exodus to Advent, 26-34; LeRoy Edwin Froom, Movement of Destiny, 541-582; and Paul A. Gordon, The Sanctuary, 1844, and the Pioneers (Washington, D C: Review and Herald Publishing Association, 1983), 85-107. Five Adventist authors offer more than a casual mention in passing of this element crucial to Andreasen's theology of the final generation; i. e., Herbert E. Douglass, ed., Perfection: The Impossible Possibility, 9-56; Herbert E. Douglass, ed., Why Jesus Waits (Washington, DC: Review and Herald Publishing Association, 1976), 11-92; John W Wood, The Sanctuary and the Atonement (Washington, DC: Review and Herald Publishing Association, 1981), 639-666, 694-729; Clinton

power to forgive in the Holy Place and God's transcendent power of abstinence from sin in the Most Holy Place, one should notice the quotation employed by Andreasen that he considered "much misunderstood."

May I read to you some paragraphs from "Early Writings," that have been perverted and misunderstood, but in the right setting have a beautiful significance. In this standard edition it is pages 54-56, "End of the 2300 Days":

'I saw a throne, and on it sat the Father and the Son. . . . Before the throne I saw the advent people,--the church and the world. I saw two companies, one bowed down before the throne, deeply interested, while the other stood uninterested and careless. Those who were bowed before the throne would offer up their prayers and look to Jesus; then He would look to His Father, and appear to be pleading with Him. A light would come from the Father to the Son, and from the Son to the praying company.'[1]

Andreasen expresses his agreement with Ellen White in

L. Wahlen, "E. J. Waggoner's Eschatology of Righteousness by Faith," M. Div. thesis, Andrews University, 1988, 40-53, 129-141, 169-186; Robert J. Wieland, The 1888 Message: An Introduction (Washington, DC: Review and Herald Publishing Association, 1980), 7-9, 92-140; and A. T. Jones, The Consecrated Way to Christian Perfection (Baker, OR: Hudson Printing Co., 1905), 113-119.

[1]Andreasen, "The Keeping Power of God," 17.

her vision and assessment as to what was occurring in the Holy Place at that particular time. He further continues his discussion:

> Now comes the end of the 2300 days, or 1844: 'I saw the Father rise from the throne, and in a flaming chariot go into the holy of holies within the veil, and sit down. Then Jesus rose up from the throne, and the most of those who were bowed down arose with Him.'[1]

Again Andreasen briefly comments in harmony with Ellen White thus far. His sence of God's need to vidicate His character and His law against Satan's accusations is evident in his understanding of the significance of Christ moving into the Most Holy Place in 1844.

> 'I did not see one ray of light pass from Jesus to the careless multitude after he arose, and they were left in perfect darkness. . . . Then a cloudy chariot . . . came to where Jesus was. He stepped into the chariot, and was borne to the holiest, where the Father sat. There I beheld Jesus, a great High Priest, standing before the Father. . . . Those who rose up with Jesus would send up their faith to Him in the holiest, and pray 'Father give us Thy Spirit'. . . . Then Jesus would breathe upon them the Holy Ghost. In that breath there was light, power, and much love, joy, and peace.'
>
> Now the picture: 'I turned to look at the company who were still bowed before the throne [in the first apartment];

[1]Ibid.

they did not know that Jesus had left it. Satan appeared to be by the throne, trying to carry on the work of God. I saw them look up to the throne [they are praying now in the first apartment], and pray, 'Father, give us Thy Spirit.' Satan would then breathe upon them an unholy influence; in it there was light and much power, but no sweet love, joy, and peace.'[1]

Entering the Most Holy Place by faith. Thus, Andreasen sees a group of people all in the Holy Place. With the fulfillment of the prophecy of Dan 8:14, the 2300 Day Prophecy (October 22, 1844), God the Father and Jesus both move from the Holy Place, where there was continuous and perpetual sin, into the Most Holy Place, where there is the blotting out of sin. Those who chose to remain in the Holy Place had made God's power of forgiveness of sin their trust, to the negation of God's higher power of abstinence from sin.

The cleansing of the heavenly sanctuary commenced with the movement, on October 22, 1844, of the Father and Jesus into the Most Holy Place where sin is to be blotted out. The cleansing of the heavenly sanctuary in Andreasenian theology is evident both in heaven and in the

[1]Ibid.

lives of God's people on earth, but only in the lives of those individuals that have their eyes fixed upon Jesus, and by faith, and faith alone, they follow and enter with Jesus into the Most Holy Place to experience, by faith, the transcendent power of God's ability, through the working of the Holy Spirit, to keep us from falling into the ugly clutches of sin. Those who remained in the Holy Place, who did not have their eyes on Christ, "the careless multitude," were left in "perfect darkness" unaware that Jesus had gone, and they continued to pray "Father give us thy Spirit." Unbeknown to this group, "Satan breathes upon them an unholy influence." Jesus does not send a single ray of light to those individuals in the Holy Place that choose to continue in sin. Therefore, all of christendom is seen in relation to the sanctuary in Andreasenian theology. An individual is either in the Holy Place, in darkness, or he/she has by faith followed Jesus into the Most Holy Place where he/she experiences the blotting out of sin or the keeping power of God. Andreasen comments:

> Christ wants us by faith to enter in with Him where He is now ministering, and there is a people that will do that. They will send up their faith to Him in the holiest of all. They will receive light and power and much joy and sweet

> peace and love. There are others who will receive light and power, but not that love which God alone can shed abroad in the hearts of His people by the Holy Spirit.
>
> Are we ready to take that step that God wants us to take? Are we ready to follow the direction given here to go with Him into the most holy, where sins are blotted out, where there is an end of sin, where transgression is finished, where reconciliation for iniquity--that means making right, restoring, clearing up the King's highway, and then bringing in everlasting righteousness--is made? . . . O that we might by faith enter with Him into that experience, and gain not only forgiveness, but that keeping power of God that will enable us, as Christ says, to go and sin no more. That is the prophetic message. That is God's message today. We must take an advanced step, or we shall be left behind in darkness in the first apartment.[1]

Andreasen perceives the moving of a people into the Most Holy Place with Christ, by faith, as vitally necessary as it relates to the accusation of Satan against God's law. In this final generation of those who by faith follow Jesus into the Most Holy Place, in them God produces people that keep His commandments without yielding to sin. Andreasenian theology is intimately tied to Andreasen's treatment of the doctrine of the sanctuary in which he clearly sets forth the importance of God's people possessing a

---

[1]Ibid.

proper understanding of the sanctuary and its cleansing of both the heavenly sanctuary and a cleansing of the people of God on earth that have moved by faith with Jesus, their High Priest, into the Most Holy Place and are living a life of victory over sin. Without this connection of Andreasen's final-generation theology in the sanctuary, his concept of the final generation would be a very weak argument. Andreasen's treatment of the sanctuary doctrine does more than just facilitate his theology of the final generation, it serves as the engine which drives Andreasenian theology.

1937 Review and Herald Article "The Eighth Commandment"

The motif of vindication

First use of the term last generation . As Andreasen proceeds chronologically, notice the theological momentum he gains building upon his established framework of the final generation. On March 18, 1937, in the Review and Herald on the Ten Commandments in his fourteenth article,[1]

[1] Andreasen, "The Eight Commandment," Review and Herald, June 24, 1937, 5-7.

under the subheading, "For Our Admonition," Andreasen states:

> This story, with all its sordid details, is written for our admonition and learning. It shows what God can do with a man who is dishonest. We have stated before that dishonesty is one of the hardest sins to eradicate from the character. But God does not want any to be discouraged. He gives us the example of Jacob, a man who had inherited tendencies which made it easy for him to be dishonest and tricky. But Jacob overcomes. He becomes Israel. He becomes the progenitor of the last generation who shall stand before the throne without spot or blemish, and in whose mouth shall be 'found no guile.'[1]

This is the first time He uses the term "the last generation," although he has been addressing the issue of the last generation, in some aspect, in his very first published works. Equally important to his first use of this term and imperative to a proper understanding at this point is Andreasen's eschatological identification of the last generation. In dealing with the eighth commandment, "Thou shalt not steal (Exod 20:15)," he turns his attention to Jacob, the supplanter:

> He was dishonest. How can God, in view of this, tell us that He is the God of Abraham, Isaac, and Jacob? The

[1]Ibid., 7.

answer is simply this: Jacob became a changed man, another man, a new man. Then his name was changed. He was no longer Jacob the supplanter, but Israel, the overcomer. He went through the night of Jacob's trouble. He suffered much--the rest of his life--but he became a new man. The old things and habits were cast aside, and though he could not escape the consequences of what he had done, God overruled all for good. His name was written in heaven, and what was done for him becomes prophetic of what God will do for the 144,000, who are the twelve tribes of Israel.[1]

Andreasen insists that Jacob's experience is prophetic and what God did for Jacob He will do for the 144,000, those who like Jacob have been changed by God, who are overcomers, who endure Jacob's time of trouble, the "twelve tribes of Israel." Now notice his definition of the last generation in his first use of the term:

> He gives us the example of Jacob, a man who had inherited tendencies which made it easy for him to be dishonest and tricky. But Jacob overcomes. He becomes Israel. He becomes the progenitor of the last generation who shall stand before the throne without spot or blemish, and in whose mouth shall be 'found no guile.' Rev. 14:5. They also are Israelites, overcomers.

[1]Ibid.

They belong to the twelve tribes.[1]

The last generation and the 144,000 synonymous . Thus, Jacob had inherited tendencies; the 144,000 and the last generation have inherited tendencies. Jacob overcame; the 144,000 and the last generation will overcome. Jacob endured his time of trouble; the 144,000 and the last generation will endure their time of trouble. Jacob's name was changed to Israel; the 144,000 and the last generation are considered to be the eschatological Israel of God, "the twelve tribes." Andreasen considers the 144,000 and the last generation as interchangeable terms, and he uses them synonymously.

Having defined and established who the last generation is he establishes another essential and critical point:

> They also are Israelites, overcomers. They belong to the twelve tribes. Many of them have been Jacobs. But that is past. God Himself can find no fault with them. 'They are without fault before the throne of God.' In them God gives the last and final demonstration of what He can do with humanity. They, like Jacob, go through the furnace of affliction. They go through 'the time of *Jacob's* trouble." Jer. 30:7. But they come out without any trace of their

[1]Ibid.

former failing. They have gained complete victory.[1]

How the final generation secures victory. How do they, the final generation, survive the furnace of affliction without being burned by sin? Andreasen emphasizes the fact that "in them God gives the last and final demonstration of what He can do with humanity."[2] It is not the final generation accomplishing this victory; it is God working in and through them demonstrating what He can do with weak sinful men that yield their wills to Him.

It is extremely important that Andreasen capitalizes upon God's strong favor for the last generation, in that he abjured those remaining in the Holy Place, because he argues that God works within the votary to demonstrate "what He can do with humanity."[3] Andreasen clarifies and reiterates the fact that it is not us, sinful humanity, accomplishing, but God Himself actively functioning in sinful humanity that produces overcomers.

This is Andreasen's theological Weltanschauung (world

---

[1]Ibid.

[2]Ibid.

[3]Ibid.

view). He perceives the magnalia Dei (mighty acts of God) as they relate to the satanic accusation that God's justice and mercy are irreconcilable and that God's law cannot be kept--retrospective eschatology. Thus, a new law of liberty is needed, which Satan claims to possess. But God had a plan that was "broader and deeper" than the single purpose of redeeming fallen, sinful humanity. What was and is paramount to God, according to Andreasen, is the "vindication of His character" and His law against the vicious claims of Satan.[1] Thus, causing the repentant believer's character to become obedient to and conformed to the law of God is the object of the heavenly mediation of Christ. However, this conformity must take place in the believers life, through the believers own volition (free will), and it must be done out of the believers love for God.

Whatever God sets out to do, that He does. God will finish His work in the earth on time. Rom 9:28. None can hinder Him. God will build His church, and the gates of hell shall not prevail against it. Matt 16:18. God, who is both he author and finisher of our faith and who has begun in us the good work, will also finish it. Heb 12:2; Phil 1:6.[2]

[1]White, Patriarch and Prophets, 68.

[2]Andreasen, Isaiah, the Gospel Prophet, 167.

While there remains a plethora of other articles written by Andreasen in the 1930s, it is the above article, the last article Andreasen writes prior to the publication of his major work on the sanctuary, The Sanctuary Service in 1937, which impacts most profoundly upon his unique theology of the final-generation.

1937 Andreasen's Book
The Sanctuary Service

Andreasen's final-generation theology reaches its fruition and climaxes in the writing of The Sanctuary Service. Every major and minor theological point written by Andreasen concerning his final-generation theology, prior to the publication of The Sanctuary Service in 1937, is drawn upon. The culmination of Andreasen's unabridged theology of the final generation is a concomitant to the doctrine of the sanctuary. As often quoted by Andreasen, the relationship between the final generation the doctrine of the sanctuary is clear in his thinking:

> The subject of the sanctuary . . . opened to view a complete system of truth, connected and harmonious, . . . Light from the sanctuary illumined the past, the present, and

the future.[1] As God's dwelling place among men, the sanctuary must ever be of deep and abiding interest to the believing child of God. When, in addition, we understand that . . . the services of the tabernacle on earth were symbolic of a higher service above, that the entire ritual and all the sacrifices on the earthly altars pointed to the true Lamb of God, the sanctuary becomes of still more importance. In it the gospel is foreshadowed and some of the deep things of God revealed. . . this work is the very essence of Christianity, the heart of the atonement.[2]

Adventist recognition and acceptance of Andreasen's major work

M. E. Kern, at that time president of the Seventh-day Adventist Theological Seminary, wrote the introduction to The Sanctuary Service and closed the introduction thus:

God has greatly blessed the author of this book in his study and teaching of these great truths, and we heartily commend this comprehensive and lucid treatise on the sanctuary service to all who desire to know the ways of God more perfectly.[3]

Between the years of 1931-1938, Andreasen was the

---

[1] White, The Great Controversy, 423.

[2] Andreasen, The Sanctuary Service, 7, 8.

[3] Ibid., 10, 11 (1937 ed. only).

president of and taught at Union College, Nebraska, during the writing and publishing of this book.[1] The year following the publication of The Sanctuary Service, Andreasen was invited to teach at the Seventh-day Adventist Theological Seminary, located at that time in Washington, D. C. He remained at the Seventh-day Adventist Theological Seminary as a professor of Biblical exegesis for eleven years.[2] Preceding the title page of this book,[3] a notation states that the content of The Sanctuary Service was "presented in lecture form at the Seventh-day Adventist Theological Seminary, and published for the 1938 Ministerial Reading Course of Seventh-day Adventists." The salient point to be made here is the fact that Andreasen had taught this message of the final generation (as published in The Sanctuary Service) for many years prior to 1938, and it was approved and accepted by leaders in the Seventh-day Adventist Church.

---

[1]A brief sketch of Andreasen's years during the 30's has been mentioned on p. 48.

[2]SDA Encyclopedia, 1975 ed., s.v. "Andreasen, Milian Lauritz"; Steinweg, Without Fear or Favor, 116-144.

[3]Andreasen, The Sanctuary Service (1937 ed. only).

The remainder of this chapter attempts to set forth clearly the teachings of M. L. Andreasen's theology of the final generation as printed in The Sanctuary Service.

Laying a consistent foundation

Although, Andreasen's theology of the final generation is seen here in its mature, developed state,[1] his first task was to lay a congenial foundation and to erect a framework consistent with the axiom developed in his previously published material. Thus, in covering this compendium of Andreasen's theology of the final generation, it is necessary to recapitulate axiomatic developments as they are observed to compare their correlative affinity.

Three basic sources[2] have supplied a wealth of information in tracing the development of Andreasen's final-

[1]This maturation of Andreasen's final-generation theology is not evident until chapter 21, "The Last Generation." Andreasen builds up to this point.

[2]Andreasen, "The Christian Life," Sabbath School Lesson Quarterly, 1924, consisting of 13 individual lessons; Isaiah, the Gospel Prophet, 1928, his commentary on the book of Isaiah; and Review and Herald articles in the years of 1926, 1936, and 1937.

generation theology to this point. The six major axioms that constitute the developed framework of Andreasenian Theology: (1) the motif of human ability to overcome sin;[1] (2) the motif of hatred for sin;[2] (3) the motif of eschatological patience;[3] (4) the motif of challenge;[4] (5) the motif of dependence;[5] and (6) the motif of vindication[6] have been identified in Andreasen's selected works prior to the publication of The Sanctuary Service, and each of them is addressed in this major work.

The opening paragraph of chapter 1 depicts God, after the fall of humanity, walking through the garden looking for man and pleading "Where art Thou?" Gen 3:9. Andreasen states that this picture is beautiful because "these are the first

[1]See pages, 35-47.

[2]See pages, 49-53, 101-105.

[3]See pages, 65-77.

[4]See pages, 79-85.

[5]See pages, 79-95.

[6]See pages, 119-120.

recorded words of God to man after the fall,"[1] and significant because God, according to Andreasen's motif of dependence,[2] is looking for humanity toward the close of earth's history in a very special way. Six verses later, God begins to prepare humanity for this special task, which concept Andreasen developed in his motif of eschatological patience.[2] " 'I will put enmity between thee and the woman, and between thy seed and her seed.' Gen 3:15."[3] Andreasen's reinterpretation of this text, "without doing violence to its meaning, would read, 'I will put hatred of sin into your heart.' This was a distinct promise of present help to Adam."[4] What did Adam, humanity-- according to Andreasen--need help with? "God would help him resist [motif of human ability to overcome sin][5] and conquer

---

[1]Ibid.

[2]See pages, 79-95.

[2]See pages, 65-77.

[3]Andreasen, The Sanctuary Service, 14.

[4]Ibid.

[5]See pages, 35-47.

[motif of eschatological patience][1] sin by placing enmity to it [motif of hatred for sin][2] in his heart."[3] He states that "Hatred of sin is vital to full salvation."[4] What does he mean by "full salvation?" Is Andreasen in fact saying that an individual cannot be saved unless he/she possesses a hatred for sin in their heart? It seems that this hatred for sin must be fully developed in those individuals that will constitute the final generation, and thus hatred for sin is vital for full salvation.

> As love of good is vital, so also is hatred of evil. It may truly be said that our capacity for love of the good is measured and balanced by our capacity for hatred of evil. . . . This combination of love and hatred must be in every Christian. They are fundamental in Christianity. It is significant that the first promise of a Saviour in the Bible is prefaced by the promise of God's help in conquering sin by giving man a capacity for hatred of evil.[5]

---

[1]See pages, 66-67.

[2]See pages, 49-53, 101-105.

[3]Andreasen, The Sanctuary Service, 14, 15.

[4]Ibid, 15.

[5]Ibid.

The problem here is that Andreasen is not addressing individual salvation. He is speaking primarily to the motif of vindication.[1] Notice the following in his previous statement, "This combination of love and hatred must be in every Christian. They are fundamental in Christianity." This is indisputably true for every child of God. Now observe the gravitational pull of Andreasen's vindication motif:

> This hatred is a great factor in our struggle with evil and our eventual victory over it. Were it not for the fact that God implants in the heart of every Christian a hatred of evil as well as a love for the right, there would be little hope for us.[2]

"Hatred is a great factor" because the final generation is "summoned in a trial. The question at issue here is: 'Who is the true God?' The nations are challenged to bring their

---

[1]The motif of eschatological patience and the motif of dependence are concomitant. Actually, the motif of vindication embraces all of the fundamental axioms that constitute the developed framework of Andreasen's final-generation theology. This is clearly evident in chapter 21 of The Sanctuary Service.

[2]Andreasen, The Sanctuary Service, 15.

witnesses."[1] This is where the motif of hatred for sin is "vital to full salvation" in his theology of the final generation. "God will bring His [witnesses]. On the testimony of these witnesses [the final generation] hangs the case."[2] Andreasen adds, "The great controversy begun in heaven was to be decided in the very world, on the very same field, that Satan claimed as his."[3] At this junction, if the members of the final generation have not cultivated, with the help of God, "a hatred of evil as well as a love for the right, there would be little hope for us."[4] For him, this little hope quickly turns to no hope, because:

> The plan of redemption had a yet broader and deeper purpose than the salvation of man. It was not for this alone that Christ came to the earth; it was not merely that the inhabitants of this little world might regard the law of God as it should be regarded; but it was to vindicate the character of God before the universe.[5]

---

[1]Andreasen, Isaiah, the Gospel Prophet, 161.

[2]Ibid.

[3]Ibid., 68, 69.

[4]Andreasen, The Sanctuary Service, 15.

[5]White, Patriarchs and Prophets, 68.

Based upon his use of the preceding statement of Ellen G. White, Andreasen seems to suggest that while the salvation of humanity is God's ultimate purpose in the plan of redemption, the issue of vindication is essential. In this sense vindication seems, for Andreasen, to be the foremost and primary purpose in the plan of salvation.

From this point forward to chapter 21, "The Last Generation," Andreasen focuses upon the first two developmental concepts of his final-generation theology, i.e., the motif of human ability to overcome sin and the motif of hatred for sin. It seems, though, from Andreasen's stated belief, that there "has been much misunderstood."[1] In nearly every chapter through to chapter 21, Andreasen augments and reiterates the motif of human ability to overcome sin along with the motif of hatred for sin, because they are vital components in Andreasenian theology--essential to the salvation of humanity.[2]

---

[1]Andreasen, "The Keeping Power of God," 17.

[2]Andreasen, The Sanctuary Service, 16-21; 49; 54, 55; 60; 62, 63, 67; 73-79, 82-84, 86-87; 90, 91; 104, 105, 110, 113-115; 121, 122; 145, 146; 166, 167; 177, 179; 192-195, 197, 209; 262, 263; 296-298.

Treatment of the sanctuary doctrine and the final-generation

Priest and prophet. Andreasen's final-generation theology as presented in chapter 21 is evident throughout his treatment of the sanctuary doctrine. His approach to the priest and the prophets of the Old Testament sanctuary and its services is from a perspective of the final generation and principles that he has already presented.

> It was God intent that every priest should have the prophetic spirit and sound the prophetic message. In God's plan it is not enough to attempt to remedy matters after a wrong has been committed. It was far better to prevent evil than to attempt to heal it. Wonderful as it is to be lifted up from sin and degradation, it is still more wonderful to be kept from falling. "Go and sin no more" is the true prophetic message. It is better to obey than to sacrifice. Every true servant of God should echo this message if he would fulfill the counsel of God.[1]

Subsequent to Andreasen's position on Satan's accusation against and challenge to God it is simply "not enough to attempt to remedy matters" for God is depending upon the final generation to be victorious, as Job was, not to

[1]Ibid., 86-87.

fail in a futile attempt. Notice his language and its affinity to the language used in his article "The Keeping Power of God:" "Wonderful as it is to be lifted up from sin and degradation, it is still more wonderful to be kept from falling."[1] The concept of humanity's mission on earth Andreasen again considers it to be the primary responsibility of God. "The work of the prophet is not done until the Lord's work in the earth is finished."[2] It is not the task of humanity, it is not their challenge, but it is the challenge of Satan to God, and it is His work to produce a people as a final demonstration of what He can do in and with humanity. This work is the sealing of the 144,000 whom He will call as His witnesses to the trial. God is depending on them as He did on Job. Upon their witness hangs the case. This work is so vital to the vindication of God's character, according to Andreasen, that it is not until "this work is done, that the end will come."[3]

Peace offerings. The peace offering is that part of the

---

[1]Ibid.

[2]Ibid., 87.

[3]Ibid.

sacrificial system where God, the priest, and the sinner commune together only after the sinner comes to sacrifice, not for sin, but for the purpose of total dedication of self, the burnt offering, and of means, the meal offering, to God.[1] Andreasen addresses the issue of vows. In this section on vows he depicts the world in a deplorable state, and yet "in the midst of all this confusion there must be, there will be, a people upon whom God can depend."[2] These are the people who have offered themselves as a living sacrifice unto God. This is the primary purpose of God's plan of redemption. "This is the supreme hour and opportunity of the Church. The world is due a demonstration that there is a people who remain faithful in a faithless generation . . . and this manifestation will reveal a people who have the seal of God's approval."[3] This demonstration is the major focus of chapter 21.

The day of atonement. It may appear rather odd that Andreasen does not provide a separate chapter on the daily

---

[1]Ibid., 116-123.

[2]Ibid., 121.

[3]Ibid., 122.

sacrifices. This fact may lead some to believe that he neglected to address this issue which deals with the theology of imputation. Andreasenian theology can be easily misunderstood to be a theology of total or extreme impartation, which is legalistic and works oriented, if it is not studied searchingly. This fact, primefacie, seems alarming, however, as recently illustrated, several books which are fundementally interested in imputation have no chapter specifically entitled the daily sacrifice. The following works are representative of this phenomenon: Biblical Research Committee of the General Conference of Seventh-day Adventist, The Sanctuary and the Atonement; Stephen N. Haskell, The Cross and Its Shadow; F. C. Gilbert, Practical Lessons; E. G. White, Christ in His Sanctuary; Edward Heppenstall, Our High Priest; W. D. Frazee, Ransom and Reunion Through the Sanctuary (Nashville, TN: Southern Publishing Association, 1977); Alfred Edersheim, The Temple; and Stephen F. Olford, The Tabernacle: Camping with God.[1] Many of them addressed

---

[1]F. C. Gilbert, Messiah in His Sanctuary (Washington, DC: Review and Herald Publishing Association, 1937), 52-59, offers a chapter on the daily offerings which is basically a compilation of Bible texts and quotes from the writings of

the daily sacrifice, as Andreasen did while discussing the Day of Atonement. Andreasen deals with the daily in several places.[1] He cites its earthly cultic use as "sacrifices for the nation 'covered' all sin done throughout Israel for that particular day. The daily sacrifice on the altar represented Christ, who died for us 'while we were yet sinners.'"[2] He also provides an application that corresponds with his compartmentalized depiction of the inner court. The daily was administrated on the Day of Atonement because it was an important part of the service. They worked together. From the daily the sinner received pardon and forgiveness, but the Day of Atonement was for the purpose of cleansing, and the sinner was cleansed from sin. Forgiveness was appropriated in the Holy Place, but the blotting out or the cleansing of sin from God's people took place only in the Most Holy Place on the Day of Atonement. Thus, those who will comprise the final generation must move with Christ, by faith, into the Most Holy Place.

E. G. White.

[1]Andreasen, The Sanctuary Service, 148, 171, 172, 176, 184, 185, and 187.

[2]Ibid., 184.

The scapegoat. This is the apologetic section of the book where Andreasen confronts the issue of Azazel making atonement on the Day of Atonement instead of the Lord's goat. In this chapter, cleansing is a major issue. Toward the end of the chapter, referring to the Day of Atonement, Andreasen states that "God shall again Cleanse His people."[1] The idea of a forensic objective cleansing and, in conjunction with it, a spiritual subjuctive cleansing of God's people on earth from sin is common in Andreasen's treatment of the doctrine of the sanctuary.[2]

These meanings of cleansed are significant in view of the fact that the subject of the sanctuary has been trodden underfoot and the truth cast to the ground. Will the time come when the subject of the sanctuary will again be give its rightful place, when God will vindicate His truth, and the error and secret machination will be uncovered? Yes, answers prophecy, the time shall come. . . . At the end of the twenty-three hundred days a people shall arise who will have light on the sanctuary question, who follow Christ by faith into the most holy, who have the solution to break the power of the mystery of iniquity, and who go forth to battle for God's truth. . . . God's people will have a part in

[1]Ibid., 209.

[2]Ibid., 175, 176, 178, 187, 209, and 296-298.

showing men the opened temple.[1]

The cultic Israelite sacrifical system, the sanctuary doctrine, the writings of Ellen G. White, and the 2,300 day prophecy (Dan 8:14) are intricate parts of Andreasenian theology; without it the final-generation theology of Andreasen would be out of place and focus. The following section considers Andreasen's developed theology in chapter 21.

A compendium of Andreasen's final generation theology

The locus classicus of Andreasenian theology. In the opening paragraph of chapter 21, "The Last Generation," Andreasen offers a brief synopsis summarizing his entire theology of the final generation. This may be considered the locus classicus of Andreasenian theology:

> The final demonstration of what the gospel can do in and for humanity is still in the future. Christ showed the way. He took a human body, and in that body demonstrated the power of God. Men are to follow His example and prove that what God did in Christ, He can do in every human

[1]Ibid., 297-298.

being who submits to Him. The world is awaiting this demonstration. (Rom. 8:19.) When it has been accomplished, the end will come. God will have fulfilled His plan. He will have shown Himself true and Satan a liar. His government will stand vindicated.[1]

Forgiveness and cleansing. In the process of confronting the issue of forgiveness and cleansing, Andreasen sharpens his focus on the motif of hatred for sin, which he firmly believes is vital for full salvation of humanity. For it is in the context of the hatred of sin[2] that he introduces a vital connection to the doctrine of the sanctuary, i.e., he presents a compartmental depiction of God's power to forgive sin--the Holy Place--and God's transcendent power of abstinence from sin--the Most Holy Place.[3]

The plan of salvation must of necessity include not only forgiveness of sin but complete restoration. Salvation *from* sin is more than forgiveness *of* sin. Forgiveness presupposes sin and is conditioned upon breaking with it; sanctification is separation from sin and indicates deliverance from its power and victory over it. The first is a means to neutralize the effect of sin; the second is a restoration

[1]Andreasen, The Sanctuary Service, 299.

[2]Andreasen, "The Keeping Power of God," 16, 17.

[3]Ibid. Also see pages, 108-119.

of power for complete victory.[1]

The motif of vindication. Andreasen says that it is a "must" of absolute "necessity" for God's plan of redemption, in which the salvation of humanity is peripheral to the vindication of His character,[2] to consist of more than mere forgiveness of sin, but the motif of challenge must be addressed. The challenge is God's law. Jesus Himself kept His own law, but is humanity able to govern itself likewise? Thus, "the first [apartment] is a means to neutralize the effect of sin; the second [apartment] is a restoration of power *for* complete victory (emphasis supplied)"[3] of Satan's challenge to God. "It is for this demonstration of what the gospel can do for a man that the world is looking."[4]

After an individual yields his/her will to God and moves by faith with Christ into the Most Holy Place, "Christ places His seal upon him. He is safe, and he is sound. God has

---

[1] Andreasen, The Sanctuary Service, 300.

[2] White, Patriarchs and Prophets, 68.

[3] Andreasen, The Sanctuary Service, 300.

[4] Ibid., 301.

finished His work in him."[1] This is the work which God began in 1844. As God was depicted in the beginning, after the fall, looking for humanity, now in the end God is looking for humanity again, yet in a very different way. Those that are sealed by God "will be subjected to every temptation, but they will not fall . . . the demonstration of the power is God's vindication."[2] Andreasen continues to build on the vindication motif with this powerful statement, "It [God's demonstration in the final generation] clears Him of any and all charges which Satan has placed against Him. In the last generation God is vindicated and Satan is defeated."[3]

The concept of Satan's defeat. Extremely crucial in Andreasenian theology is the point at which Satan is defeated. He was defeated in every way specifically as it relates to that phase of Christ's work, the second phase, in

---

[1]Andreasen, The Sanctuary Service, 302.

[2]Ibid., 302, 303.

[3]Ibid., 303, 304.

Andreasen's trichotomy of atonement.[1] "In the remnant Satan *will* " meet his defeat (emphasis supplied).[2] Andreasen in reference to the cross says, "The voice of God is heard proclaiming that justice is satisfied. Satan is vanquished."[3] But, yet, he did not quit. Andreasen makes the following observation:

> He [Satan] had failed in his conflict with Christ, but he might yet succeed with men. So he went to 'make war with the remnant of her seed, which keep the commandments of God, and have the testimony of Jesus Christ.' Rev. 12:17. If he could overcome them he might not be defeated.[4]

---

[1]Andreasen uses the term defeated in its broadest sense, in that he employs to a concept of phase atonement. He says that there are "three phases in Christ's work of atonement. In the first phase he met sin face to face and conquered it. In not one instance did He fail; not one stain of sin sullied His pure soul. His body-temple was holy, a fit place for God to dwell. This stage terminated before Gethsemane. . . . The second phase included Gethsemane and Golgotha. . . . In the third phase Christ demonstrates that man can do what He did, with the same help He had." Andreasen, The Book of Hebrews, 59.

[2]Ibid., 315.

[3]Ibid., 232.

[4]Ibid., 310.

Andreasen points out why Satan attacks the remnant who keep the commandments of God. Satan believes that he still has a chance to triumph. This assumed last chance for triumph is based upon Satan's hope to vitiate God's vindication of His character and government--His law.

> The demonstration which God intends to make with the last generation on earth means much, both to the people and to God. . . . Yet, to produce a people that will keep the law is the task which God has set Himself and which He expects to accomplish.[1]

This statement supports his motif of dependence. God has made it a task for Himself to accomplish, that is, the manifestation of a people that perfectly keeps His law out of love for Him. God has chosen to make Himself dependent upon the final generation, as He did with Job, which emerges out of His acceptance of Satan's challenge:

> 'No one can keep the law. It is impossible. If there be any that can do it or that have done it, show them to me. Where are they that keep the commandments?' God will quietly answer, Here they are. 'Here are they that keep the commandments of God, and the faith of Jesus.' Rev. 14:12. Let us say it

[1]Ibid.

reverently: God must meet Satan's challenge.[1]

Andreasen's motif of challenge is retroactive; that is, he sees God as challenged by Satan's accusations prior to the creation of earth or humanity and, simultaneously, has a tenacious effect upon God's vindication.

The weakest of the weak. A very interesting perspective is introduced by Andreasen concerning those that are sealed, which constitute the final generation.

> It is not God's plan, or a part of His purpose, to subject men to tests that only a chosen few can survive. In the Garden of Eden, God subjected Adam and Eve to the lightest test conceivable. . . . And even if Satan offered them the fruit, they need not take it. But they took it and ate. And they ate it because they wanted to, not because they had to. They deliberately transgressed. There was no excuse. God could not have devised an easier test.[2]

Andreasen makes a very valid and decisive point. Adam and Eve had no excuse to yield to Satan's temptation other than willful consent. They possessed the power to overcome this temptation to disobey God's command. Continuing in the same vain of thought he states:

---

[1]Ibid., 310, 311.

[2]Ibid., 311.

> When God commands men to keep His law, it does not serve the purpose He has in mind to have only a few men keep it, just enough to show it can be done. It is not in line with God's character to pick outstanding men of strong purpose and superb training, and demonstrate through them what He can do. It is much more in harmony with His plan to make His requirements such that even the weakest need not fail, so that none can ever say that God demands that which can be done by only a few.[1]

In the new perception of the final generation, and in God's purpose, a new dimension is added to the motif of vindication. As to the necessity of the final generation, Andreasen explains:

> It is for this reason that God has reserved His greatest demonstration for the last generation. This generation bears the results of accumulated sins. If any are weak, they are. If any suffer from inherited tendencies, they do. If any have an excuse because of weakness of any kind, they have. If, therefore, these can keep the commandments, there is no excuse for anyone in any other generation not doing so also.[2]

What an indictment this brings upon all humanity. There is not one single excuse for any individual in any age to have yielded to sin. Andreasen says that it goes even further:

---

[1]Ibid., 311, 312.

[2]Ibid., 312.

> But this is not enough. God intends in His demonstration to show, not merely that ordinary men of the last generation can successfully pass a test such as He gave to Adam and Eve, but that they can survive a test much harder than such as falls to the lot of common men. It will be a test comparable to the one Job passed through, and approaching that which the Master underwent. It will test them to the utmost.[1]

Andreasen immediately turns his attention to the test of Job.[2] Recounting Job's experience, "God will produce not only one or two who keep His commandments, but a whole group spoken of as the 144,000."[3] They constitute the final generation.

The motif of challenge. Andreasen digresses to reemphasize the motif of challenge as he begins to bring his argument to a close. Within this motif is the issue of Satan's

---

[1]Ibid.

[2]Andreasen basically provides an expanded recapitulation of the Job experience in his earlier articles, i.e., [Andreasen], "Patience," 23-25; "Morning Devotional," 23-26. Cf. pages 65-86.

[3]Andreasen, <u>The Sanctuary Service</u>, 315.

accusations,[1] which he says "in reality constitute an impeachment [of God]. . . . It threatened the very existence of God's government."[2] The closing scene is that of a courtroom. He pictures God as being on trial with His government at stake: "In order for God to sustain His contention, it is necessary for Him to show . . . that it [His law] is Holy, just, and good, and that men can keep it. . . . On this God has staked His government."[3]

God can call upon many as witnesses from ages past but, according to Andreasen, Satan objects to this and calls them special, out-of-the-ordinary cases. Satan claims that God interfered in these cases, such as Job. He says "God has pampered them, and that he, Satan, has not had free access to them. If he were given full permission to press his case, they also would be won over."[4] God is a fair, just, and merciful God. In order to silence the father of all lies,

---

[1]Recapturing the weight of the accusation aids the depiction of the vindication and its magnitude.

[2]Ibid.

[3]Andreasen, The Sanctuary Service, 316.

[4]Ibid., 317.

"God removes His spirit from the earth. Satan will have a greater measure of control than he has ever had before."[1] Andreasen explicitly says that the withdrawal of God's spirit from the earth is a withdrawal from the wicked, not from the last generation, otherwise they would not stand a fighting chance in the time of trouble against Satan.[2] Satan's only restriction is, as in the case of Job, he is not being allowed to take their lives. God then goes so far as to hide Himself from His people as He hid Himself from his Son, Jesus Christ, on the cross.[3] God effectively hides Himself from the final generation by closing the heavenly sanctuary. This is a time when "the saints cry out day and night for deliverance, but He [God] appears not to hear."[4] Nonetheless, these, the weakest of the weak, possess the

---

[1]Ibid.

[2]Ibid, 318. "He provides them with food, shields them from destruction, and supplies grace and power for holy living." This power which is provided by God to the last generation is the power of the Holy Spirit working in and through them to accomplish the His biding.

[3]White, The Desire of Ages, 753-756.

[4]Ibid., 317, 318.

attitude that they would rather die than sin against the God that they love so much. It is the working of the Holy Spirit that enables the final generation to succeed.

> Satan knows what is at stake. It is now or never.[1] He numbers the world as his subjects; but the little company [the final generation] who keeps the commands of God are resisting his supremacy. If he [Satan] could blot them from the earth, his triumph would be complete.[2]

Satan's final chance. Andreasen obviously sees Satan as having a final chance to triumph over God and win the controversy. Notice carefully the Sitz im leben (back drop or setting). The chronological setting is of the essence. Two major points are: (1) God has withdrawn His Holy Spirit from the worldlings; and (2) Jesus has ceased mediation in the heavenly sanctuary. Therefore, probation for all the world is closed (Rev 22:11). Satan, most of all, "knows what is at stake."[3] Why is it now or never for Satan? How is it if Satan could blot them, God's final

---

[1]Ibid., 317.

[2]White, Great Controversy, 618.

[3]Andreasen, The Sanctuary Service, 317.

generation, from the earth, that is cause them to sin,[1] his triumph would be complete? What would be the consequences of such a triumph for Satan? Andreasen's answers to these three questions manifest his theology of the final generation in its fully matured zenith.

(1) Why is it now or never for Satan? The "never" for Satan is obvious. The "now" refers to Satan's last chance for victory, which exists in his possibility to cause the final generation to yield to sin.

(2) How is it, if Satan can blot them from the earth, that is, cause them to sin, his triumph would be complete? When Christ ceases His mediation in the heavenly sanctuary, the universal proclamation is given "He that is unjust, let him be unjust still: and he which is filthy, let him be filthy still: and he that is righteous, let him be righteous still: and he that is holy, let him be holy still" (Rev 22:11). Therefore, the righteous, in the eyes of God, living on earth are those of the

---

[1]Andreasen equates Satan's attempt to "blot them from earth" first with causing them to "yield to his temptatioins and turn from their allegienace to God" (<u>Great Controversy</u>, 618-619), which would result in their physical destruction (Ibid.).

final generation, all others have taken the mark of the beast.[1] Thus, if Satan could cause the final generation to sin, there would be no one else left on earth for God to use to refute the accusations of Satan. Then Satan would triumph.

(3) What would be the consequences of triumph for Satan? Andreasen employs the following quote in his very first publishedwork:[2]

> The foe in the wilderness had confronted Christ, assailed Him now with fierce and subtle temptations. Had Jesus yielded for a moment, had He changed His course in the least particular to save Himself, Satan's agencies would have triumphed, and the world would have been lost.[3]

The connection made by Andreasen is the association of two additional concepts, triumph and loss. Satan's triumph is equated with the loss of salvatioin for all of humanity, not just the fainal generation, according to Andreasen. Without us [the final generation], it is impossible that they [all who

---

[1]Cf. Rev 13.

[2]See pages, 62-65.

[3][Andreasen], "Obedience," 7,8.

rest in Christ since Abel][1] should be made perfect in Christ Jesus.

Andreasenian atonement. The loss of all humanity Andreasen sees as a viable possibility contingent upon the fall of God's manifested final generation. He draws on a very powerful statement of Ellen G. White. "The intercession of Christ in man's behalf in *the sanctuary above is as essential* to the plan of salvation *as was His death upon the cross.* By His death He began that work which after His resurrection He ascended to complete in heaven" (emphasis supplied).[2] This statement clearly shows Ellen G. White's

---

[1]See Heb 11:39, 40, and compare the antecedent of "they" with Heb 11:4-36, and the "they" of Heb 11:37, 38, with the "they" of Heb 11:39, 40.

[2]Steinweg, Without Fear or Favor, 169. This quote used by Andreasen is taken from, White, The Great Controversy, 489. "M. L. knew that Ellen White had used the phase, 'the benefits of His atonement,' to refer to Chirst's work in heaven. But he also knew that in the same book she had written, 'As the priest entered the most holy once a year to cleanse the earthly sanctuary, so Jesus entered the most holy of the heavenly, at the end of the 2300 days of Daniel 8, in 1844, to make a final atonement for all who could be benefited by His mediation, and thus to cleanse the sanctuary." Steinweg, Without Fear or Favor, 168.

support of a two phase atonement. Andresen does not consider this concept of the cross a devaluation of the life, death, or the resurrection of Christ. Based upon his reading of Ellen G. White, Andreasen developed the following three-phase atonement concept:

> There are thus three phases in Christ's work of atonement. In the first phase He met sin face to face and conquered it. In not one instance did He fail; not one stain of sin sullied His pure soul. His body-temple was holy, a fit place for God to dwell. This stage terminated before Gethsemane.
>
> The second phase included Gathsemane and Golgotha. There the sins which He had met and conquered were placed upon Him, that He might bear them up the cross and annul them, this being the meaning of 'put away,' in Hebrews 9:26. In the first phase He bore sins for the purpose of conquering them and eliminating them from the life. In the second phase He bore sins for the purpose of suffering and dying for them, that in His 'death he might destroy him that had the power of death, that is, the devil.' Heb. 2:14.
>
> In the third phase Christ demonstrates that man can do what He did, with the same help He had. This phase includes His session at the right hand of God, His high priestly ministry, and the final exhibition of His saints in their last struggle with Satan, and their glorious victory. Then the death sentence, which was first pronounced upon the serpent in the garden, long delayed, will be carried out.[1]

Andresen's trichotomous anatomy of atonement

[1] Andreasen, The Book of Hebrews, 59.

facilitates his theology of the final generation.[1] In his first

---

[1]This three-phase perspective of Chirst's atonement is Andreasenian. E. G. White. mentions two phases of Christ work, "He fulfilled one phase of His priesthood by dying on the cross for the fallen race. He is now fulfilling another phase by pleading before the Father the case of the repenting, believing sinner, presenting to God the offerings of His people." "The Atonement," SDA Bible Commentary, 7A: 686. "If we affirm a completed atonement in Ellen White's thought (as we must) and likewise a continuing atonement (as we must), we inevitably involve ourselves in the nature of the two and the nature of their relationship. In what sense is the atonement completed at the cross, and in what sense then is anything left to be completed: Ellen White herself speaks, as we have noted, of both a completed and a continuing atonement; but contemporary Adventist apologist frequently make a distinction between 'sacrifice'--what the incarnate Christ did on the cross--and 'atonement'--what the ascended Christ began doing in 1844. . . . Her [E. G. White] framework requires a truly completed, a continuing, and a yet-future millennial and post-millennial atonement. How past and present atonement, and present and future atonement, while separate from one another, complete one another, is part of the originality of her position. Since there is even today some sensitivity in Adventism to speaking of the atonement as completed at the cross, it should be stressed that in dealing with the *forensic aspect only* Ellen White agrees that the atonement is finsihed." Wallenkampf, The Sanctuary and the Atonement, 719. John W. Wood continues this discussion in the remainder of his article.

phase of atonement Jesus met sin face to face and conquered it. Had Jesus failed, humanity would have been lost. Andreasen adpoted this concept from Ellen G. White, "Could one sin have been found in Chirst, had He in one particular yielded to Satan to escape the terrible torture, the enemy of God and man would have triumphed."[1] Andreasen's second phase of atonement included Gethsemane and Golgotha. There the sins which He had met and conquered in phase one were place upon Him, that He might bear them up to the cross and annul them. Sin can never be "forgiven without the sacrifice on Calvary. The death of Christ is necessary for our salvation."[2] But, says Andreasen, "The cross in and of itself saves no one. It only provides salvation."[3] The writings of Ellen G. White substantiate the concept that in the Garden of Gethsemane or on the cross if Christ would have failed, humanity would have been lost.[4] The third phase of atonement Andreasen is

---

[1]White, The Desire of Ages, 761.

[2]Andreasen, The Sanctuary Service, 152.

[3]Ibid., 214.

[4]Ibid., 741-764.

depicted as being absolutely essential to God's primary plan of redemption, that is, the vindication of His character (he adopted this view from White, Patriarch and Prophets, 68). Ellen G. White supports this third phase of Andreaen, "The intercession of Christ in man's behalf in the sanctuary above is as esseential to the plan of salvation as was His death upon the cross. By His death He began that work which after His resurrection He ascended to complete in heaven."[1] Andreasen's three-phase atonement does not seem to be in conflict with the writings of Ellen G. White and differs only in that he has called that part of the life of Christ prior to the Gethsemane phase one. In each phase there exist the possibility and probability of the failure of Christ and, consequently, the loss of all humanity. But, Andreasen insists that "whatever God sets out to do, that He does. God will finish His work in the earth on time. Rom. 9:28. None can hinder Him."[2]

Andreasen closes his argument of the final generation and its connection within the sanctuary in chapter 21

[1]White, Great Controversy, 489.

[2]Andreasen, Isaiah, the Gospel Prophet, 167.

with the follwing observations:

The matter of greatest importance in the universe is not the salvation of men, important as they may seem. The most important thing is the clearing of God's name from the false accusations made by Satan. The controversy is drawing to a close. God is preparing His people for the last great conflict. Satan is also getting ready. The issue is before us and will be decided in the lives of God's people. . . .[1] The cleansing of the sanctuary in heaven is dependent upon the cleansing of God's people on earth.[2] How important, then, that God's people be holy and without blame! In them every sin must be burned out, so that they will be able to stand in the sight of a holy God and live with the devouring fire. 'Hear, ye that are far off, what I have done; and, ye that are

[1]Having fully yielded their wills, God's people are used by Him in this last great demonstration of what He, God, can do in and through mankind. It is not God's people accomplishing this last demonstration, but it is God accomplishing, by the power of the Holy Spirit, in and through His people.

[2]The cleansing of the heavenly sanctuary is considered to be the objective, and forensic cleansing work of God in the heavenly sanctuary. The subjective or practical aspect of this cleansing which takes place in the heavenly sanctuary, according to Andreasen, is the cleansing of the soul temple of God's people on earth. This cleansing of God's people on earth is inseperable from the work of the High Priest, Jesus Christ, in the Most Holy Place of the heavenly sanctuary. The cleansing of the former is what produces the condition of the latter.

near, acknowledge My might. The sinners in Zion are afraid; fearfulness hath surprised the hypocrites. Who among us shall dwell with the devouring fire? Who among us shall dwell with everlasting burnings? He that walketh righteously, and speaking uprightly; he that despiseth the gain of oppressions, that shaketh his hands from holding of bribes, that stoppeth his ears from hearing of blood, and shutteth his eyes from seeing evil; he shall dwell on high: his place of defence shall be the munitions of rocks: bread shall be given him; his waters shall be sure.' Isa. 33:13-16. . . . God is depending upon us as He did upon Job. Is His confidence well placed?[1]

Thus, if God should fail in vindicating Himself by not producing a people--the final generation--that can, out of love, keep His law, then all humanity would be lost without the third and last phase of Andreasen's concept of atonement being satisfied. This concept constitutes the whole matter of Andreasen's final-generation theology.

This concludes the descriptive perspective of this study and the articulation of the chronological development of M. L. Andreasen's final-generation theology and its connection in his treatment of the doctrine of the sanctuary. The following and final chapter turns to the concluding thoughts of this thesis.

---

[1]Ibid., 320, 321.

CHAPTER III

THE SANCTUARY AND THE FINAL GENERATION: CONCLUSIONS AND EPILOGUE

> Whatever God sets out to do, that He does. God will finish His work in the earth on time. No one can hinder Him.
>
> M. L. Andreasen[1]

From the outset of this study, several questions were asked regarding the development of Andreasen's final-generation theology and the possibility, within his theology, of the final generation being expected to precipitate the ultimate vindication of God by means of character perfection. The search for answers to the inquiries has demanded the careful chronological analysis of all published and unpublished writings of Andreasen.[2] Having completed the chronological analysis of Andreasen's life's work, it is possible to address the mentioned inquiries from a

---

[1] Andreasen, Isaiah, The Gospel Prophet, 167.

[2] See pages,36-39.

descriptive perspective. The evidence provided by the analyses of the material permits the following conclusions.

Conclusions

Concerning the question of whether any major or critical theological metamorphosis occurs in the development of Andreasen's final-generation theology between the years 1924 and 1937, this study concludes that from his very first published work to the fruition of his final-generation theology Andreasen is precise, and consistant in the development of his final-generation theology and its relation to the doctrine of sanctuary.

The methodology Andreasen employs is, fundamentally, a Biblical approach. He substantiates his position via systematic deduction and Biblical exegesis. He attempts to develop his final-generation theology virtually on Biblical evidence alone. Outside of the fourth quarter Sabbath School lessons of 1924, "The Christian Life," which are comprised largely Ellen G. White material, Andreasen rarely quotes her writings. However his use of her material is very evident . Andreasen's endeavor to support his theology solely on Biblical evidence is thwarted by his apparent retrospective theological focus. He constantly and consistantly focuses upon the controversy which took place in heaven, prior to the creation of this world, between Christ and Satan. The latter's accusation against God's law--that it is impossible for humanity to keep the law out of love--is the veritable polestar of Andreasenian theology. His detailed knowledge of this account is the result of his dedicated study of the writings of Ellen G. White.[1] The Bible offers basically three references concerning Satan prior to the creation of this world: Isa 14:12-21, Ezk 28:11-19, Rev 12:1-4. From these three Biblical references alone it seems impossible that Andreasen could have comphrended his retrospective vindication motif without the knowledge and the support of the writings of Ellen G. White.

The controversial issue of the nature of Christ within Adventism today is not a concern of Andreasen as many might be lead to believe consequential to his focus upon the final-generation. Christology is important to Andreasen and is vital to his three phase atonement concept, but within the

---

[1]White, Desire of Ages, 24; Patriarchs and Prophets, 33-51; Story of Redemption, 13-41.

area of Christology the nature of Christ goes unaddressed. However, Andreasen does confront the issue of perfection. Perfection seems to be an overcoming of known, willful, and presumptuous sin. It is not the eradication of the sinful nature of man, nor is it the attainment of a nature equal with that of Christ. For Andreasen character perfection is basically an attitude.

The fourth quarter Sabbath School lessons of 1924, "The Christian Life," consisting of thirteen lessons; the "Morning Devotional Study: Patience of the Saints; Commandments of God; the Faith of Jesus"; and Isaiah, the Gospel Prophet are the only three documents of the 1920s written by Andreasen yielding information pertinent to this research. Of these three, the first two are the very first documents Andreasen ever published.[1] Within these three documents is found what is believed to be the very

---

[1]To my knowledge, only five published items are to be considered: "The Christian Life," the fall quarter Sabbath School lessons of 1924; "Morning Devotional Study: Patience of the Saints; Commandments of God; the Faith of Jesus"; "Minnesota's Best Soul-Winning Year," Review and Herald, April 7, 1927; Isaiah, the Gospel Prophet; and "Daniel and Religious Liberty," Review and Herald, March 21, 1929.

framework upon which Andreasen builds his final-generation theology.

In "The Christian Life," Lesson 2, on "Righteousness by Faith," Andreasen develops the point that Christ kept the law, which was a demonstration of human beings' ability to obey God's law. Apparent in this development is Andreasen's reference back to the original controversy in heaven between God and Satan, in which Satan makes railing accusations against God, His character, and His law. These accusations of Satan basically indict God and charge His law as being impossible to keep. Thus, Andreasen focuses on the life of Christ as "a demonstration of the possibility of keeping the law" by fallen humanity. In addition, Christ offered "the righteousness of that life to anyone who will receive it; that the life also of Jesus might be made manifest in our body, and that we might be made the righteousness of God in Him."[1] The concept of the imparted righteousness of Christ is evident in Andreasen's following remarks:

The law requires righteousness,--a righteous life, a perfect character; and this man has not to give. He can not

[1] [Andreasen], "Righteousness by Faith," 4-6.

meet the claims of God's law. But Christ, coming to the earth as man, lived a holy life, and developed a perfect a character. These He offers as a free gift to all who will receive them. His life stands for the life of men.[1]

In Lesson 3, of this same series, Andreasen addresses the issue of "obedience." The focus of this lesson is the idea of obedience resulting from the love of God and not the fear of God. This perspective is not an unorthodox view in the Seventh-day Adventist Church, but the significance of this tenet is not the orthodoxy of Andreasen's view, rather, significance is seen in the origin of this perspective. This view finds its referent in the controversy between God and Satan in heaven as described by E. G. White.[2] In this lesson, Andreasen casually employs a statement of E. G. White's, without any immediate comment, which later becomes a vital aspect in his final-generation theology: "Had Christ yielded for a moment, had He changed His course in the least particular to save Himself, Satan's agencies would

---

[1]Ibid., 5.

[2]White, Patriarchs and Prophets, 38-42.

have triumphed, and the world would have been lost."[1]

Lesson 10 introduces Andreasen's idea of biblical patience and the work of humanity on earth. Both of these ideas are thoroughly expounded in his "Morning Devotional Study: The Patience of the Saints; Commandments of God; the Faith of Jesus." The framework upon which Andreasen builds his theology of the final generation, at least to this point, is evident in this article. At the center of his attention is the challenge of Satan to God, and "God depending upon us." In this article, as in each article mentioned, his theology is retrospective to the controversy in heaven between God and Satan.

The last source to be chronologically considered for the 1920s was Andreasen's commentary of the book of Isaiah. He further reemphasizes the concept of patience in the light of the banner carried by the final generation as their testimony of obedience to God's commandments.[2] Following this point, he hammers the last nail into the developmental framework of his final-generation theology.

---

[1] [Andreasen], "Obedience," in "The Christian Life," 7-8.

[2] Andreasen, Isaiah the Gospel Prophet, 161.

Depicting the universe as a court room with God being on trial, Andreasen focuses upon four major points: (1) his concept of challenge, Satan challenging God; (2) patience, the steadfast endurance of the final generation; (3) human beings' work on earth, humanity's vital share in the vindication of God; and (4) dependence, the case of God's ultimate vindication hanging on the testimony of the final generation. Thus, in the material considered, the developmental framework of Andreasenian theology has been clearly uncovered and its relationship within the sanctuary doctrine has been set forth.

In establishing the lines of the development of Andreasen's theology of the final generation, the 1920s and the years of 1930-1937 are regarded as particularly illuminating, as Andreasen's theology takes significant form. Only two articles, mentioned below, are considered relevant to the development of his final-generation theology in the 1930s. In these two articles, he gains theological momentum as he builds upon his established framework of the final generation from the 1920s.

In the article, "The Keeping Power of God," the basic thrust is the development of the motif of hatred for sin, which Andreasen mentioned in his first Sabbath School lessons series. He states that "It is just as important to learn to hate sin as it is to learn to love righteousness. . . ."[1] He depicts the hatred of sin as being a vital necessity in God's plan of redemption. In order for one to experience God's keeping power, one must possess a hatred for sin.

Andreasen displays a strong desire to protect the doctrine of forgiveness from perversion. He champions the cause. There is no doctrine in the Bible that is more precious to Andreasen than the doctrine of the forgiveness of God. That is why a hatred for sin is vital to Andreasenian theology. God graciously grants His forgiveness to the record of His children, but the moment they become satisfied with God's forgiveness this satisfaction becomes their crutch, and as such becomes a perversion of the doctrine of forgiveness.[2]

The delineation of his concept of God's keeping power is set forth in his compartmentalized depiction of God's

---

[1]Andreasen, "The Keeping Power of God," 16.

[2]If I may be evaluative at this point it seems as though the apostle Paul confirms this concept in his comments recorded in Rom 6:1-2: "What shall we say then? Shall we continue in sin, that grace may abound? God forbid. How shall we, that are dead to sin, live any longer in it?"

power to forgive sin (the Holy Place) and of God's transcendent power of abstinence from sin (the Most Holy Place). Andreasen clearly reveals in his application of the sanctuary doctrine its connection and place in his theology of the final generation. He displays character perfection as a goal for all Christians. He sees character perfection as the overcoming sin in this life and, more importantly, he describes this character perfection as a prerequisite for those who comprise the final generation.

In Andreasen's article on "The Eight Commandment," he employs, for the first time, the term "the last generation." He capitalizes upon God's puissant predilection for the last generation. Andreasen clarifies and forcefully reiterates the fact that it is not sinful humanity accomplishing something, but, rather, God Himself actively living and functioning in sinful humanity, that He, God, produces the last generation. The last generation consists only of those individuals who attain character perfection, are sealed, and who, by faith, move with Jesus into the Most Holy Place. According to Andreasen, this is the little company, the small flock, and the 144,000 that God has placed His confidence in. They will endure the time of trouble such as never was. Andreasen declares that because God has reproduced the character of His Son Jesus Christ in them perfectly, they possess the attitude whereby they would rather die than sin against the God they love. What is of great significance here is the fact that in Andreasen's theology, the final generation possesses the Holy Spirit in its fullness after Christ leaves the Most Holy Place. This is the post-probationary time of trouble when the Spirit of God is withdrawn from the earth. This withdrawal of the Spirit of God must be a withdrawal from the wicked. Andreasen is very explicit on the point that the ability of the final generation to triumph in the post-probationary time of trouble is the work of the Spirit of God in them. It was God's self-given task as a point of vindicating Himself before the universe from the railing accusations of Satan.

There are six basic axioms that constitute the developed framework of Andreasen's theology of the final generation, which are brought to The Sanctuary Service, where his theology is found in its matured state. These six points are: (1) the motif of human beings' ability to overcome sin, (2) the motif of hatred for sin, (3) the motif of eschatological patience, (4) the motif of challenge, (5) the motif of dependence, and (6) the motif of vindication. Andreasen uses the first twenty chapters to lay a congenial foundation consistent with these six axiomatic concepts. He especially focuses upon the motif of human beings' ability to overcome sin and the motif of hatred for sin throughout the first twenty chapters.

Andreasen's treatment of the sanctuary doctrine and his theology of the final generation are inseparable. By his study of the priests and the prophets of the sanctuary , Andreasen concludes that the true prophetic message that is to be delivered today is "go and sin no more." When this message has been preached and the Lord has finished His work in the earth, then the end will come. The peace offerings depict those who have fully dedicate themselves to God and experience true communion. They have kept their vow and God will use them for the final demonstration to the world of what He can do in and through humanity. The Day of Atonement is dealt with in respect to the daily oblation, the morning and evening sacrifices. The daily offers forgiveness, but cleansing of the sanctuary and of God's people came only on the Day of Atonement. In the chapter on the scapegoat, Andreasen addresses the issue of the cleansing of the sanctuary. This cleansing is the blotting out of sin in the lives of God's people, of those who move with Him into the Most Holy Place. The end of the 2,300 day prophecy of Dan 8:14 began this cleansing process and it is God's self-given task to bring forth a people that constitute the final generation and thus vindicate His government and character.

In chapter 21, "The Last Generation," Andreasen's theology of the final generation reaches its zenith. It is capsulated in the opening paragraph of chapter 21, the locus classicus of Andreasenian theology:

> The final demonstration of what the gospel can do in and for humanity is still in the future. Christ showed the way. He took a human body, and in that body demonstrated the power of God. Men are to follow His example and prove that what God did in Christ, He can do in every human being who submits to Him. The world is awaiting this demonstration. (Rom. 8:19.) When it has been accomplished, the end will come. God will have fulfilled His plan. He will have shown Himself true and Satan a liar. His government will stand vindicated.[1]

Andreasen discloses the eschatological impact and significance of his theology of the final generation and its

---

[1] Andreasen, The Sanctuary Service, 299.

connection with the ultimate defeat of Satan and the ultimate vindication of God. It is very evident in Andreasen's theology that the concept of complete atonement for all humanity, as well as the ultimate vindication of God, is completed in a series of events or phases, not in one particular event, mainly the cross. He espouses a trichotomus anatomy of the atonement, which he derive from the writings of Ellen G. White. The death of Christ on the cross of Calvary, which is the second phase of atonement, is emphasized as the all-important necessary phase, by Andreasen, but it does not constitute a complete atonement process, per se, in its broadened definition in this concept of the atonement for humanity. Furthermore, the second phase of the atonement does not vindicate God's claims concerning the possibility of keeping His law.

The possibility and probability of failure by Christ exists in his three-phase atonement which would result in the loss of the entire human race. Andreasen does not see any devaluation of Christ's death or resurrection. In fact, the most distinctive concept in Andreasenian theology as seen from this perspective is that God must answer the accusations of Satan in order to vindicate Himself before the universe. Andreasen argues that the vindication of God is paramount to the salvation of human beings. Thus, if God should fail in producing a people, the final generation (phase three of Andreasen's atonement) that can stand in the time of trouble (which is strictly for the purpose of testing the final generation), then Andreasen insists that God cannot save humanity. If such a failure were to occur, the consequence would be the loss of all of humanity, which includes all people from Abel to the present.

The comforting aspect of Andreasenian theology is the fact that God does not fail. Just as Christ could have failed in the Garden of Gethsemane, and all of humanity would have been lost, the same contingency of failure exists in the final generation. But, likewise, the same Christ of Gethsemane exists in the final generation, and He shall be victorious in them as He personally was victorious in the Garden. This vision represents Andreasen's theology of the final generation at its zenith and in full maturity.

Implications for Further Study

This understanding of Andreasen's theology of the final

generation raises questions to be considered for further study: What views were held by Seventh-day Adventists in the mid-1800s to the early 1900s concerning the final generation? What is the perceived understanding of Andreasen's theology of the final generation by Seventh-day Adventists at the time of the publication of The Sanctuary Service? What are the implications of Andreasenian theology for Seventh-day Adventist Theology today? In other words, what is the status and cogency of Andreasenian theology today? These questions are important in view of the fact that Andreasen taught in the Adventist Theological Seminary for eleven years, and in light of the fact that his book on the sanctuary was used to train ministers in the doctrine of the sanctuary in North America for some time. However, what is currently taught and accepted as traditional Seventh-day Adventist theology concerning the sanctuary is dissimilar on selected points of eschatology (the study of the end-time events), soteriology (the science of salvation), hamartiology (the science of sin), and the vindication of God in comparison with aspects of the theology presented by Andreasen. These questions indicate areas of fruitful, critical, and evaluative investigations of Andreasen's theology of the final generation and its connection in the treatment of the doctrine of the sanctuary.

SELECTED BIBLIOGRAPHY

Books Authored by M. L. Andreasen

Andreasen, M. L. The Book of Hebrews. Washington, DC: Review and Herald Publishing Association, 1948.

________. The Faith of Jesus and the Commandments of God. Washington, DC: Review and Herald Publishing Association, 1939, 1949.

________. A Faith to Live By. Washington, DC: Review and Herald Publishing Association, 1943.

________. Following the Master. Nashville: Southern Publishing Association, 1947.

________. Isaiah, the Gospel Prophet, A Preacher of Righteousness; Lesson Notes and Helps. 3 vols. Washington, DC: Review and Herald Publishing Association, 1943; reprint, Payson, AZ: Leaves of Autumn Books, 1981, 1985, 1986.

________. Letters to the Churches, Series A. Payson, AZ: Leaves of Autumn Books, 1980, 1982, 1983, 1984, 1985, 1986.

________. Man--Here and Hereafter. Mountain View, CA: Pacific Press Publishing Association, 1937.

________. Prayer. Mountain View, CA: Pacific Press Publishing Association, 1957.

________. The Sabbath: Which Day and Why? Washington, DC: Review and Herald Publishing Association, 1942.

________. Saints and Sinners. Washington, DC: Review and Herald Publishing Association, 1951.

________. The Sanctuary Service. Washington, DC: Review and Herald Publishing Association, 1947.

________. What Can a Man Believe? Mountian View, CA: Pacific Press Publishing Association, 1951.

Articles Authored by M. L. Andreasen

Andreasen, M. L. "The Atonement." 15 February 1957. Ellen G. White Research Center. Andrews University.

________. "The Atonement." 4 November 1957. Ellen G. White Research Center. Andrews University.

________. "Atonement IV ." 14 November 1957. Ellen G. White Research Center. Andrews University.

________. "Atonement VII." 19 January 1958. Ellen G. White Research Center. Andrews University.

________. "Atonement VIII: Bloodless Atonement." 31 January 1958. Ellen G. White Research Center. Andrews University.

________. "The Atonement IX." 13 March 1958. Ellen G. White Research Center. Andrews University.

________. "The Book of Hebrews--No. 3: The Message of the Book." Review and Herald, 3 October 1946, 7, 8.

________. "The Book of Hebrews--No. 5: Christ's Atoning Work." Review and Herald, 24 October 1946, 9, 10.

________. "The Christian and the Sanctuary: The Message of the Book of Hebrews." Signs of the Times, 12 November 1949, 10-14.

________. "The Christian Life," in Sabbath School Lesson Quarterly, Pacific Press Publishing Association, 1924.

________. "The Eighth Commandment." Review and Herald, 24 June 1937, 5-7.

________. "The Importance and Content of Hebrews." Review and Herald, 19 September 1946, 6, 7.

________. "The Intent of the Sacrificial System." Ministry, July 1939, 22-23, 27, 45.

________. "The Keeping Power of God." Review and Herald, 18 June1936, 16, 17.

________. "The Laodicean Message and Righteousness by Faith." Review and Herald, 9 November 1939, 6-8.

________. "The Ministry of Our High Priest." Review and Herald, 11 October 1945, 5, 6.

________. "Morning Devotional Study: Patience of the Saints; Commandments of God; the Faith of Jesus." Review and Herald, 18 June 1926, 23-26.

________. "A Most Dangerous Heresy." N.d. Ellen G. White Research Center. Andrews University.

________. "The Sanctuary." Review and Herald, 19 October 1944, 10-13, 66, 67.

________. "The Sanctuary--No. 1: Priests and Levites." Review and Herald, 19 September 1940, 3-5.

________. "The Sanctuary--No. 2: Consecration and Dedication" Review and Herald, 26 September 1940, 4-6.

________. "The Sanctuary--No. 3: The Ram of Consecration." Review and Herald, 3 October 1940, 7-8.

________. "The Sanctuary--No. 4: Dedication and Inauguration--Part I." Review and Herald, 10 October 1940, 4-5.

________. "The Sanctuary--No. 5: Dedication and Inauguration--Part II." Review and Herald, 17 October 1940, 4-6.

________. "The Sanctuary--No. 6: The Daily Sacrifice--Part I." Review and Herald, 24 October 1940, 5-7.

________. "The Sanctuary--No. 7: The Daily Sacrifice--Part II." Review and Herald, 31 October 1940, 4-6.

________. "The Sanctuary--No. 8: The Sin Offering." Review and Herald, 14 November 1940, 6-8.

________. "The Sanctuary--No. 9: Defilement and Blood." Review and Herald, 21 November 1940, 8-10.

________. "The Sanctuary--No. 10: The Day of Atonement." Review and Herald, 28 November 1940, 18-19.

________. "The Sanctuary--No. 11: The Work of Judgment." Review and Herald, 12 December 1940, 6-8.

________. "The Sanctuary--No. 12: The High Priet as Sin Bearer." Review and Herald, 19 December 1940, 5-6.

________. "The Sanctuary--Part I: The Tabernacle in the Wilderness." Review and Herald, 18 October 1945, 6-8.

________. "The Sanctuary--Part II: The Daily Services." Review and Herald, 18 October 1945, 6-8.

________. "The Sanctuary--Part III: The Burnt Offering." Review and Herald, 18 October 1945, 6-8.

________. "The Sanctuary--Part IV: Meat and Peace Offerings." Review and Herald, 18 October 1945, 6-8.

________. "The Sanctuary--Part V: The Lesson of the Sin Offerings--No. 1." Review and Herald, 18 October 1945, 6-8.

________. "The Sanctuary--Part VI: The Lesson of the Sin Offerings--No. 2." Review and Herald, 18 October 1945, 6-8.

________. "The Sanctuary--Part VII: The Lesson of the Sin Offerings--No. 3." Review and Herald, 18 October 1945, 6-8.

________. "The Sanctuary--Part VIII: The Day of Atonement--No. 1" Review and Herald, 18 October 1945, 6-8.

________. "The Sanctuary--Part IX: The Day of Atonement--No. 2." Review and Herald, 18 October 1945, 6-8.

________. "The Sanctuary--Part X: Concerning the Scapegoat." Review and Herald, 18 October 1945, 6-8.

________. "What Is Man?" These Times, 28 April 1958, 7.

________. "Why I Believe in the Second Coming of Christ: God's Timetable Will Not Fail." Signs of the Times, 2 January 1951, 5-6, 15.

All Other Sources

Adams, Roy. The Sanctuary Doctrine: Three Approaches in the Seventh-day Adventist Church. Andrews University Seminary Doctoral Dissertation Series. Vol. 1. Berrien Springs, MI: Andrews University Press, 1981.

Andreasen, Neils-Erik. "The Sanctuary Doctrine and the Church's Mission." Review and Herald, 16 Feburary 1984, 6-8.

Andrews, J. N. "The Order of Events in the Judgment." Nos. 1-20. Signs of the Times, 3 January 1878 - 31 October 1878, 7.

________. "The Sanctuary and Its Cleansing." Review and Herald, 30 October 1855, 68, 69.

________. "Watchman, What of the Night?" Review and Herald, 27 May 1852, 14-16.

Andross, Elmer E. A More Excellent Ministry. Mountain View, CA: Pacific Press Publishing Association, 1912.

Aulén, Gustaf. Christus Victor: An Historical Study of the Three Main Types of the Idea of Atonement. Translated by A. G. Hebert. New York: Maxmillan Publishing Co., 1969.

Bacchiocchi, Samuele. An Analysis of Robert Brinsmead's Teaching Regarding the Cleansing of the Sanctuary. New York: Faith for Today, 1963.

Bates, Joseph. "The Laodicean Church." Review and Herald, November 1850, 21-24.
Battistone, Joseph J. "Why the Day of Atonement Merits Our Attention." Review and Herald, 10 March 1983, 8-9.

Baumgärtel, Friedrich. "The Hermeneutical Problem of the Old Testament," Essays on Old Testament Hermeneutics, 34-159. Edited by Claus Westermann. Eng. trans. James L. Mays. Richmond, VA: John Knox Press, 1963.

Blazen, Ivan T. "Judgment and Assurance" Review and Herald, 4 August 1983, 5-6.

________. "The Tension Resolved." Review and Herald, 11 August 1983, 7-10.

Brinsmead, Bernard H. "The Sanctuary in Adventist Theology from Approximately 1840-1850." Term paper, Andrews University, 1975.

Burton, R. G. "The Sanctuary and the Blotting Out of Sins." Ministry, March 1972, 35-37.

________. "The Sanctuary and the Blotting Out of Sins." Ministry, April 1972, 31-33.

Butler, George I. "At the Time Appointed the End Shall Be." Review and Herald, 12 November 1908, 8, 9.

________. "At the Time Appointed the End Shall Be--No.2." Review and Herald, 3 December 1908, 9, 10.

________. "The Certainty and the Triumph of the Advent People." Review and Herald, 19 November 1908, 7, 8.

________. "Many Voices--No. 1: Early Beginnings." Review and Herald, 17 August 1911, 3, 4.

________. "Many Voices--No. 2: Earlier and Later Movements." Review and Herald, 24 August 1911, 3-5.

________. "Many Voices--No. 3: The Sanctuary Service." Review and Herald, 31 August 1911, 4, 5.

________. "Many Voices--No. 4: Positive Evidence that Christ Did Minister in the First Apartment of the Heavenly Sanctuary after His Ascension." Review and Herald, 7 September 1911, 3, 4.

________. "Many Voices--No. 5: Further Proof of Christ's Ministry in the First Apartment of the Heavenly Sanctuary after His Ascension." Review and Herald, 14 September 1911, 5, 6.

________. "Many Voices--No. 6: The Judgment and the Judgment Message; the Cleansing of the Sanctuary or the Work of Judgment at the End of the 2300 days." Review and Herald, 21 September 1911, 4, 5.

Calvin, John. Concerning the Eternal Predestination of God. London: James Clarke and Co., 1961.

Canale, Fernando Luis. "A Criticism of Theological Reason: Time and Timelessness as Primordial Presuppositions." Ph.D. dissertation, Andrews University, 1983.

Chadwick, Samuel. The Call to Christian Perfection. Kansas City: Beacon Hill Press, 1943.

Coffman, Carl. Unto a Perfect Man. Berrien Springs, MI: Andrews University Press, 1969, 1982.

Corliss, J. O. "The Atonement--No. 1: Its Nature and Object." Review and Herald, 22 June 1916, 7, 8.

________. "The Atonement--No. 2: The Motive Benind It." Review and Herald, 29 June 1916, 7, 8.

________. "The Atonement--No. 3: The Agency Involved." Review and Herald, 6 July 1916, 9.

________. "The Atonement--No. 4: The Manifestation of Divine Love." Review and Herald, 13 July 1916, 7.

________. "The Atonement--No. 5: Its Heavenly Mediation." Review and Herald, 20 July 1916, 8, 19.

________. "The Atonement--No. 6: Recognized by Patriarchs." Review and Herald, 27 July 1916, 5-6.

________. "The Atonement--No. 9: Some Steps Toward its Accomplishment." Review and Herald, 24 August 1916, 8, 9.

________. "The Atonement--No. 10: Its Significance to the Work at Large." Review and Herald, 31 August 1916, 6, 7.

________. "The Atonement--No. 11: The Weighing of Character." Review and Herald, 7 September 1916, 9, 10.

Cottrell, Raymond F. "The Antitypical Day of Atonement." Editorials. Review and Herald, 25 February 1965, 13; 4 March 1965, 15; and 11 March 1965, 12, 13.

Couperus, Molleurus. "The Bible Conference of 1919: The Use of the Spirit of Prophecy in Our Teaching of Bible and History." Spectrum 10, no. 1 (1979): 23-57.

Damsteegt, P. Gerard. Foundations of the Seventh-day Adventist Message and Mission. Berrien Springs, MI: Andrews University Press, 1988.

Davidson, Richard M. Typological Structures in the Old Testamaent and New Testament. Berrien Springs, MI: Andrews University Press, 1981.

________. "Righteousness by Faith in the Sanctuary Typology of the Pentateuch." Research paper. September 1975.

De La Potterie, Ignace. "L'Impeccabilitè du Chrétien d'après I John 3, 6-9." In L'Evangile de Jean: Etudes et Problèmes, 161-177. Edited by F. M. Braun. Lovanii: Desclée de Brouwer, 1958.

Douglass, Herbert E. The End: Unique Voice of Adventists About the Return of Jesus. Mountian View, CA: Pacific Press Publishing
Association, 1979.

________. "Importance of the Sanctuary Truth." Editorals. Review and Herald, 4 September 1975, 13; 18 September 1975, 13, 14; 2 October 1975, 12, 13; 23 October 1975,10, 11.

________, ed. Perfection: The Impossible Possibility. Nashville: Southern Publishing Association, 1975.

________ , ed. Why Jesus Waits. Washington, DC: Review and Herald Publishing Association, 1976.

Doukhan, Jacques. "The Seventy Weeks of Daniel 9: An Exegetical Study." Andrews University Seminary Studies 17 (Spring 1979): 1-22.

Dybdahl, Jon. "The Sanctuary as a Call to Moral Seriousenss." Spectrum 14, no. 3, (1983): 52-55.

Edersheim, A. The Temple, Its Ministry and Services as They Were at the Time of Jesus Christ. Grand Rapids, MI: Eerdmans, 1976.

Edwardson, C. "The Judgment." Review and Herald, 10 July 1930, 13-15.

Eichrodt, Walther. "Typological Exegesis an Appropriate Method?" Essays on Old Testament Hermeneutics. Edited by James L. Mays. Richmond, VA: John Knox Press, 1963.

Ford, Desmond. Daniel 8:14: The Day of Atonement and the Investigative Judgment. Casselberry, FL: Euangelion Press, 1980.

Frazee, W. D. Ransom and Reunion Through the Sanctuary. Nashville: Southern Publishing Association, 1977.

________ . "Then Shall the Sanctuary Be Cleansed." Seventh-day Adventist Annual Council Devotional Message, 1974. Review and Herald, 6 March 1975, 4-6.

French, T. M. "The Atonement and the Judgment." Review and Herald, 12 December 1935, 4, 5.

________. "Judgment Hour Message." Review and Herald, 5 December 1935, 7, 8.

Froom, LeRoy E. Movement of Destiny. Washington, DC: Review and Herald Publishing Association, 1971.

________. The Prophetic Faith of Our Fathers: The Historical Development of Prophetic Interpretation. 4 vols. Washington, DC: Review and Herald Publishing Association, 1950-1954.

Fulton, J. E. "Corroboration of Sanctuary Positions." Ministry, June 1938, 9, 10.

"Genesis." The Pulpit Commentary. Edited by H. D. M. Spence and Joseph S. Exell. Grand Rapids, MI: Eerdmans Pub. Co., 1980. 1:79.

Gilbert, F. C. "The Anointing of the Anti-typical Most Holy." Ministry, August 1934, 3, 4.

________. Messiah in His Sanctuary. Washington, DC: Review and Herald Publishing Association, 1937.

________, ed., Practical Lessons. Nashville: Southern Publishing Association.

González, Justo L. A History of Christian Thought. New York: Abingdon Press, 1975.

________ . The Sanctuary, 1844, and Pioneers. Washington, DC: Review and Herald Publishing Association, 1983.

Gordon, Paul A., ed. Pioneer Articles: On the Sanctuary, Daniel 8:14, The Judgment, 2300 Days, Year-day Principle, Atonement 1846-1905. Ellen G. White Research Center. Andrews University. Berrien Springs, MI, 1983.

Gulley, Norman R. Christ Our Substitute. Washington, DC: Review and Herald Publishing Association, 1982.

Haddock, Robert. "A History of the Doctrine of the Sanctuary in the Advent Movement, 1800-1905." B. D. thesis, Andrews University, 1970.

Hardinge, Leslie. Outline Studies of the Sanctuary. Payson, AZ.: Leaves of Autumn Books, 1987. (Reprint.)

Hasel, Gerhard F. "Blood and Old Testament Sacrifice: Cleansing and Defilement by Blood." Research paper. N.d., Ellen G. White Research Center. Andrews University. Berrien Springs, MI.

________ . Old Testament Theology: Basic Issues in the Current Debate. Grand Rapids, MI: Eerdmans Publishing Co., 1972.

________ . Understanding the Living Word of God. Mountain View, CA: Pacific Press Publishing Association, 1980.

Haskell, S. N. The Cross and Its Shadow. Washington, DC: Review and Herald Publishing Association, 1949.

________ . "The Nature of Judgment." Review and Herald, 24 October 1912, 5, 6.

Hauser, Robert. Give Glory to Him: The Sanctuary in the Book of Revelation. Angwin, CA: Robert W. Hauser, M.D. 1983.

________ . Daniel, Revelation and the Final Generation. Angwin, CA: Morningstar Ministries, 1987.

Haynes, Carlyle B. The Hour of God's Judgment. Mountain View, CA: Pacific Press Publishing Association, 1926.

________ . "Sanctuary and Its Cleansing." Review and Herald, 17 January 1935, 4-6.

Heppenstall, Edward. Our High Priest: Jesus Christ in the Heavenly Sanctuary. Washington, DC: Review and Herald Publishing Association, 1972.

Holbrook, Frank B., ed. Symposium on Daniel, Daniel and Revelation Committee Series. Vol. 2. Washington, DC: Biblical Research Institute, 1986.

________ . "Does the Judgment Jeopardize Assurance?" Review and Herald, 22 July 1982, 6-8.

________ . "Light in the Shadows: An Overview of the Doctrine of the Sanctuary." Research paper.

________ . "The Sanctuary and Assurance." Review and Herald, 15 July 1982, 4-5.

________. 70 Weeks, Leviticus, Nature of Prophecy, Daniel and Revelation Committee Series. Vol. 3. Washington, DC: Biblical Research Institute, 1986.

________. "Walking in the Light: An Overview of the Doctrine of Salvation in Christ." Research paper.

Holt, Benjamin R. "A Comparative Study of the Sanctuary and Its Implications for Atonement in Seventh-day Adventist Theology from Uriah Smith to the Present." Term paper, Andrews University, 1969.

Howell, W. E. "V. Forgiveness in the Light of Sanctuary." Ministry, June 1942, 35, 36.

________. "VI. Why God Waits to Finalize on Sin." Ministry, July 1942, 35, 36.

________. "VII. In the Time of Patient Waiting." Ministry, August 1942, 35-37.

Jemison, T. Housel. A Prophet among You. Mountain View, CA: Pacific Press Publishing Association, 1955.

Johns, Varner J. "The Hour of His Judgment Is Come." Review and Herald, 9 July 1964, 8, 9.

Jones, Alonzo T. The Consecrated Way to Christian Perfection. Baker, OR: Hudson Printing Co., 1905.

Kerr, Hugh Thomson. A Compendium of Luther's Theology. Philadelphia, PA: Westminster Press, 1943.

LaRondelle, Hans K. Perfection and Perfectionism: A Dogmatic Ethical Study of Biblical Perfection and Phenomenal Perfectionism. 2nd ed. Berrien Springs, MI: Andrews University Press, 1975.

Larson, Ralph. "A Test and a Sign." Review and Herald, 31 December 1981, 4-7.

Litch, Josiah. "The Ten Virgins." Advent Herald and Signs of the Times Messenger, 21 May 1845, 120.

Loucks, Clarence Melvin. "The Theological Foundations of the Victorious Life: An Evaluation of the Theology of the Victorious Christian Life in the Light of the Present and Future Aspects of Biblical Sanctification." Ph.D. dissertation, Fuller Theological Seminary, 1984.

Lucas, Richard L. "Considerations of Method in Old Testament Hermeneutics." The Dunwoodie Review 6 (1966): 7-66.

Maxwell, C. Mervyn. God and His Sanctuary. Mountain View, CA: Pacific Press Publishing Association, 1980.

________. God Cares: The Message of Daniel. 2 vols. Mountain View, CA: Pacific Press Publishing Association, 1981.

________. Tell It to the World: The Story of Seventh-day Adventists. Mountain View, CA: Pacific Press Publishing Association, 1976.

Muller, Richard A. Dictionary of Latin and Geek Theological Terms Drawn Principally from Protestant Scholastic Theology. Grand Rapids, MI: Baker Book House, 1985, 1986.

Naden, L. C. "Christ's Atoning Ministry: What Does It Do for Us in the Judgment?--1." Review and Herald, 10 September 1964, 2-4.

________. "Christ's Atoning Ministry--2. Christian Perfection: How Do We Attain It?" Review and Herald, 17 September 1964, 2-4.

Neall, Beatrice S. The Concept of Character in the Apocalypse with Implications for Character Education. Washington, DC: University Press of America, 1983.

Neufeld, Donald F. "A Basis of Confidence - 1" Review and Herald, 21 Feburary 1980, 14-15.

________. "A Basis of Confidence - 2" Review and Herald, 28 Feburary 1980, 17-18.

________. "Can Forgiveness Ever Be Canceled?" Review and Herald, 20 May 1971, 13.

________. "The Investigative Judgment - 1" Review and Herald, 7 Feburary 1980, 13-14.

________. "The Investigative Judgment - 2" Review and Herald, 14 Feburary 1980, 13-15.

________. "No Sanctuary, No True Adventism." Review and Herald, 9 November 1978, 10-21.

________ . "Thy Way. . . Is in the Sanctuary." Review and Herald, 6 November 1969, 13, 14.

________ . "Was the Atonement Finished on the Cross?" Review and Herald, 22 April 1976, 11, 12.

________ , ed. Seventh-day Adventist Encyclopedia. Rev. ed. Washington, DC: Review and Herald Publishing Association, 1976.

Nichol, F. D. Answers to Objections: An Examination of the Major Objections Raised Against the Teachings of Seventh-day Adventists. Washington, DC: Review and Herald Publishing Association, 1932.

________ , ed. Seventh-day Adventist Bible Commentary. 7 vols. Washington, DC: Review and Herald Publishing Association,1953-1957.

Olson, A. V. "The Judgment in Heaven." Ministry. November 1963, 18-21.

Olson, Robert W. "An Historical Survey of Seventh-day Adventist Statements on the Doctrine of the Cleansing of the Heavenly Sanctuary." Prepared for the Sanctuary Review Committe, 1980. Ellen G. White Estate, Washington, DC.

________ . "The 1919 Bible Conference and Bible and History Teachers' Council." Ellen G. White Reasearch Center. Andrews University. Berrien Springs, MI.

Onjukka, Lauri. The Sanctuary and Perfection. Temecula, CA: Lifemark Press, 1982.

Ott, Helmut. Perfect in Christ. Washington, DC: Review and Herald Publishing Association, 1987.

Owen, R. S. "The Sanctuary and Its Cleansing." Review and Herald, 26 March 1925, 11-20.

Peck, Sarah Elizabeth. The Path to the Throne of God: The Sanctuary or the Gospel According to Moses. Angwin, CA: Educational Frlt Aids, 1976.

Pelikan, Jaroslav. The Christian Tradition: A History of the Development of Doctrine. Chicago, IL: The University of Chicago Press, 1971.

Read, W. E. "Studies on the Sanctuary--No. 1: God's Plan and Purpose." Review and Herald, 25 August 1932, 795-97.

________. "Studies on the Sanctuary--No. 2: The Earthly and Heavenly Sanctuary." Review and Herald, 8 September 1932, 846-48.

________. "Studies on the Sanctuary--No. 3: Christ Our Great High Priest." Review and Herald, 15 September 1932, 871-73.

________. "Studies on the Sanctuary--No. 4: Order of Service in the Heavenly Sanctuary." Review and Herald, 22 September 1932, 895-97.

________. "Studies on the Sanctuary--No. 5: Christ Ministers in Both Apartments of the Heavenly Sanctuary." Review and Herald, 29 September 1932, 918-19.

________. "Studies on the Sanctuary--No. 6: What the Daily Service Accomplished." Review and Herald, 6 October 1932, 944-46.

________. "Studies on the Sanctuary--No. 7: The Cleansing of the Sanctuary." Review and Herald, 13 October 1932, 969-71.

________. "Studies on the Sanctuary--No. 8: The Final Disposal of Sin." Review and Herald, 20 October 1932, 992-93.

________. "Studies in the Sanctuary--No. 9: The Hour of Judgment." Review and Herald, 27 October 1932, 1017-18.

________. "Studies on the Sanctuary--No. 10: The Time of the Third Angel's Message." Review and Herald, 3 November 1932, 1040-41.

Rice, M. Leslie. From Disappointment to Victory. Washington, DC: Review and Herald Publishing Association, 1949.

Rupp, E. Gordon, and Philip S. Watson. The Library of Christian Classics: Luther and Erasmus: Free Will and Salvation. Philadelphia, PA: Westminster Press, 1953.

Schwarz, Richard W. Light Bearers to the Remnant: Denominational History Textbook for Seventh-day Adventist College Classes. Mountain View, CA: Pacific Press Publishing Association, 1979.

Seventh-day Adventists Answer Questions on Doctrine: An Explanation of Certain Major Aspects of Seventh-day Adventist Belief. Washington, DC: Review and Herald Publishing Association, 1957.

Seventh-day Adventist Bible Commentary. 10 vols. Edited by F. D. Nichol. Washington, DC: Review and Herald Publishing Association, 1955.

Seventh-day Adventists General Conference Biblical Research Committee. The Brinsmead Agitation: Its Background, Attitudes, and Some of Its Teachings. Washington, DC: Review and Herald Publishing Association, 1969.

Seventh-day Adventists General Conference Biblical Research Committee. The Sancturay and the Atonement: Biblical, Historical, and Theological Studies. Washington, DC: Review and Herald Publishing Association, 1981.

Shea, William H. Daniel and the Judgment. Washington, DC: Biblical Research Institute, 1980.

________ . Selected Studies on Prophetic Interpretation, Daniel and Revelation Committee Series. Vol. 1. Washington, DC: Review and Herald, 1982.

Shuler, John L. The Great Judgment Day in the Light of the Sanctuary Service. Washington, DC: Review and Herald Publishing Association, 1952.

Smith, Preston. "How Shall We Stand." Review and Herald, 6 March 1969, 9, 10.

Smith, Uriah. Daniel and Revelation. Washington, DC: Review and Herald Publishing Association, 1944.

Standish, Colin D., and Russel R. Standish. Adventism Unveiled. Rapidan, VA: Historic Truth Publications, 1984.

Steinweg, Virginia. Without Fear or Favor. Washington, DC: Review and Herald Publishing Association, 1979.

Strand, Kenneth A. "The Victorious-Introduction Scenes in the Visions in the Book of Revelation." Andrews University Seminary Studies 25 (1987): 267-269.

Venden, Morris. From Exodus to Advent. Washington, DC: Review and Herald Publishing Association, 1980.

Waggoner, J. H. "The Atonement." Nos. 1-21. Signs of the Times, 25 May 1876-26 October 1876.

________ . The Atonement in the Light of Nature and Revelation. Mountain View, CA: Pacific Press Publishing Association, 1884.

Wahlen, Clinton L. "E. J. Waggoner's Eschatology of Righteousness by Faith." M. Div. thesis, Andrews University, 1988.

Wallenkampf, Arnold V., ed. The Sanctuary and the Atonement, Vol. 1, Biblical Studies. Washington, DC: Review and Herald Publishing Association, 1980.

Waterhouse, Douglas. "Understanding the Sanctuary." Syllabus for a Course on the Sanctuary, Andrews University, 1974.

Watson, C. H. The Atoning Work of Christ, His Sacrifice and Priestly Ministry. Washington, DC: Review and Herald Publishing Association,1934.

________. "The Cleansing of the Sanctuary." Review and Herald, 14 March 1935, 12-14.
________. "The Investigative Judgment." Review and Herald, 7 March 1935, 3, 4.

________. "The Sanctuary in Heaven." Review and Herald, 21 February 1935, 10, 11.

Weber, Martin. Some Call It Heresy. Washington, DC: Review and Herald Publishing Association,1985.

Wieland, Robert J. The 1888 Message: An Introduction. Washington, DC: Review and Herald Publishing Association, 1980.

Wieland, Robert J., and Donald K. Short. 1888 Re-Examined. Leominster, MA: Eusey Press, 1987.
Wiggers, H. W. The Ford Issue and the Sanctuary Debate. Payson, AZ: Leaves of Autumn Books, 1983. (Reprint.)

White, Ellen G. Christ in His Sanctuary. Mountain View, CA: Pacific Press Publishing Association, 1969.

________. Christ's Object Lessons. Washington, DC: Review and Herald Publishing Association, 1941.

________. The Desire of Ages. Mountain View, CA: Pacific Press Publishing Association, 1940.

________ . Early Writings of Ellen G. White. Washington, DC: Review and Herald Publishing Association, 1945.

________ . Education. Mountain View, CA: Pacific Press Publishing Association, 1903.

________ . Evangelism as Set Forth in the Writings of Ellen G. White. Washington, DC: Review and Herald Publishing Association, 1946.

________ . The Great Controversy Between Christ and Satan During the Christian Dispensation. Washington, DC: Review and Herald Publishing Association, 1950.

________ . Maranatha. Washington, DC: Review and Herald Association, 1976.

________ . Selected Messages. Washington, DC: Review and Herald Publishing Association, 1958.

________ . Steps To Christ. Washington, DC: Review and Herald Publishing Association, 1892.

________ . The Story of Prophets and Kings as Illustrated in the Captivity and Restoration of Israel. Mountain View, CA: Pacific Press Publishing Association, 1943.

________ . The Story of Redemption. Washington, DC: Review and Herald Publishing Association, 1947.

________ . The Story of Patriarchs and Prophets as Illustrated in the Lives of Holy Men of Old Mountain View, CA: Pacific Press Publishing Association, 1958.

________ . Testimonies to the Church. 9 vols. Mountain View, CA: Pacific Press Publishing Association, 1948.

________ . Testimonies to Ministers and Gospel Workers. Mountain View, CA: Pacific Press Publishing Association, 1923, 1944, 1962.

White, James. "The Angels of Revelation XIV." Review and Herald, 29 November 1853, 164.

________ . "The Judgment." Review and Herald, 29 January 1857, 100.

________ . The Judgment. Oakland, CA: Pacific Press Publishig Co., 1891.

________ . "The Parable, Matthew XXV, 1-12." Review and Herald, 9 June 1851, 97-103.

________ . "This Generation." Signs of the Times, 4 June 1874, 6.

________ . A Word to the "Little Flock." Facsimile reproduction. Washington, DC: Review and Herald Publishing Association, 1944.

White, Stephen S. Five Cardinal Elements in the Doctrine of Entire Sanctification. Kansas City: Beacon Hill Press, 1949.

Wolfkill, Guy F. "The End of the Great Controversy between Christ and Satan as Described in the Books of Daniel and the Revelation." A paper presented to the Bible Research Fellowship, Angwin, California, 1952. Adventist Heritage Center. James White Library. Andrews University.

Wood, John W. The Sanctuary and the Atonement. Washington, DC: Review and Herald Publishing Association, 1981.

Zurcher, Jean. La Nature de L' Homme. Paris: Presses Universitaires de France, 1962